That Peculiar Affirmative

On the Social Life of Poems

That Peculiar Affirmative

On The Social Life of Poems

Jonathan Farmer

STEPHEN F. AUSTIN STATE UNIVERSITY PRESS

Stephen F. Austin State University Press
PO Box 13007, SFA Station
Nacogdoches, TX 75962
sfapress@sfasu.edu
936-468-1078

For information about special discounts for bulk purchases, please contact:
Texas A&M University Press Consortium
tamupress.com
800.826.8911

ISBN: 978-1-62288-472-8
Book design by Sarah Johnson

For links to all the poems discussed in the book visit
https://www.thatpeculiaraffirmative.net/

Contents

To Caroline

Introduction

Poems are social. One person writes a poem hoping another person will read it. I read it differently if I know that a computer assembled it. I read it differently if I know that a person wrote it by creating a set of rules that, computer-like, generated the poem independent of any subsequent personal will or awareness of others—of me. On the other hand, even a poem written by a person to resist assumptions about communication is a kind of communication; it implies awareness of the person it might resist.

But a poem isn't social in the way that my sitting down to dinner with you would be. Neither is this book. I write "you" without knowing exactly who that is or how or if or through what medium it might reach you. If you read it, you read it without the obligations that would come with seeing me, and I write it without the obligations or opportunities that being with you, knowing you, would entail.

I'm curious about the social life of poems. Not so much the one involved in a poem's clumsy, half-commercial transit from one person to another, though I'd love to read someone's book about that. Rather, I'm interested in the social life that individual poems embody and enact. To what extent, I wonder, can poems embody the virtues we cherish in our actual social lives? A poem speaks to a reader it cannot imagine, however much and however poignantly a poem like "Crossing Brooklyn Ferry" tries. Time and place do avail. Distance avails. In reading I listen to—listen for—a poet whose presence in that moment is reconstituted in my own voice, whose very achievement of a continuous moment is part of its artifice. And yet.

There are some poems that not only feel kind to me but make me feel as if I am a recipient of their kindness. There are poems in which the apparent humility of the poem seems akin to humility outside of a poem, manifesting both humility's benefits and, in some cases, its limitations. There are poems in which the encounter with another person, in spite of my invisibility to that person, entails some of the same complexities and rewards as my encounters with others in actual, physical proximity to me. And there are cases in which the difference between the encounter in a poem and the encounter in what we frequently call "real life" can show us something about real life.

Among the things that poems can't do is code switch. They can't speak differently depending on the person they're talking to. They can't change the subject or talk differently because I am grieving today or I am shot through with delight. They can't hear that I recently changed my medication and require some patience. And in that way, poems do imagine us—or misimagine us. And we are of course free to walk away from them because it is the wrong moment or because this poem expects you to be someone you are not, because it assumes you are not biracial, say, not queer, not poor, and for better or worse that walking away will mean less. It will mean almost nothing at all. The poem, the poet, will never know.

In putting forward a particular set of virtues in this book I do not mean to suggest that they're cardinal virtues—or even that they are always virtues—in our social or poetic lives. Among my interests here is defining some of the ways that poetry can interact with these supposed virtues, which have frequently encoded stereotypes of race, ethnicity, class, ability, and gender. Especially in the case of decorum, a term that has fallen out of favor because it so often enforces cultural and linguistic hierarchies, I wanted to see how those same virtues could instead be employed to envision the boundaries they previously enforced.

Just as much as our social life encodes cultural forces, though, it also operates within our individual tastes and tendencies. And so this book about social life is also, inevitably, a book about myself. I've tried to be open about the times when my personal presence in these encounters dictates the kind of experience I describe, and have tried, too, to see beyond my limitations when applicable. But those limitations persist: These essays are case studies, and it is myself that I have enlisted as their subject. That means that my personal taste determines what poems come under consideration, as does the subject itself. Pretty much every poem I discuss in this book presents a coherent speaker. I don't intend to argue for my taste, any more than I would want to argue for my personality. Instead, I've tried to use these particular poems to get a clearer (or, at least, more detailed) image of what it means—what it might mean—for one person to encounter another through this particular, imperfect medium that is itself as various as the humanity it hopefully serves. Its service, writ large, of humanity is a function of this poem's service to this person, in this moment, and I—an often-anxious, middle-aged man, one who learned to trust poems at a time when he hadn't yet learned to trust people; one who has sometimes found in poems evidence that life matters (found ways of imagining my own life as mattering) when otherwise incapable of imagining that; one who, like many people who grew up inside my particular, massive constellation of demographic and personal good fortunes, only belatedly learned to see how fortunate he was—I am at the heart of it.

In the process of trying to map the rich, unlikely relationships that occur between imperfectly imagined poet and unimaginable reader, I've also tried to refine my understanding of those forces that inform, enliven, resist and reshape our encounters with each other, and in particular of those forces' relationship to an American society that is, collectively, only now learning (and more recently, it seems, once again refusing) to recognize the diversity that was already written into it, though in different terms, at the first moment a Florentine explorer and cartographer unknowingly lent two continents, spanning the distance between the Arctic and Antarctic circles, a version of his name. By that time, in the early 1500s, two centuries had already passed since another man from what we now think of as Italy wrote sonnets that would, a few decades after Vespucci died, help to shape the early incarnations of poetry in what we now call Modern English, including a handful of poems that I teach to my 10th grade students at the beginning of every year.

That span thrills me in much the same way that glimpses of distant galaxies thrill some of my friends. And that thrill rekindles in those moments when I, speaking through the poems, and the poems, speaking through me, manage to span the distances between some of those students and me. That the materials of our connection are not only the words we speak, with their own archaeological complexity, and the forms the poems inhabit, revise, and reject, but also the elements of life, including despair, makes our connection, and the pleasure I feel in it, more complicated, and more reassuring, too, just as in friendship it is the ability to accommodate and sometimes transform sorrow that often makes the friendship most viable. In her long, slow, patient poem "The Moose," itself the product of 20 years of intermittent writing and thought, Elizabeth Bishop refers to this, or something like it, as "that / peculiar affirmative":

> The passengers lie back.
> Snores. Some long sighs.
> A dreamy divagation
> begins in the night,
> a gentle, auditory,
> slow hallucination....
>
> In the creakings and noises,
> an old conversation
> —not concerning us,
> but recognizable, somewhere,
> back in the bus:
> Grandparents' voices
>
> uninterruptedly
> talking, in Eternity:
> names being mentioned,
> things cleared up finally;
> what he said, what she said,
> who got pensioned;

deaths, deaths and sicknesses;
the year he remarried;
the year (something) happened.
She died in childbirth.
That was the son lost
when the schooner foundered.

He took to drink. Yes.
She went to the bad.
When Amos began to pray
even in the store and
finally the family had
to put him away.

"Yes ..." that peculiar
affirmative. "Yes ..."
A sharp, indrawn breath,
half groan, half acceptance,
that means "Life's like that.
We know *it* (also death)."

Talking the way they talked
in the old featherbed,
peacefully, on and on,
dim lamplight in the hall,
down in the kitchen, the dog
tucked in her shawl.

It is, characteristically, deliberately, a modest image of social life, one seen from without ("an old conversation / —not concerning us"). And it is the best description I have for what poems sometimes do for me—that unlikeliness, that affirmation, that sense, for however long we can keep it alive, that a viable "we" exists. Out of that, I have tried to make something worth your time.

"Praise the Mutilated World": On Joy

What does a joyous poem say about, say to, a world in which many feel despair? If you and I are together and care about each other, the joy of one might be a gift to the other, though you or I would likely dim that same joy if the other was suffering, out of care for the other's feelings. My joy might feel, if I expressed it then, like indifference—and joy is, to some extent, indifferent, an all-in bodily sense of being possessed by the goodness and gift of things. (Which is why, on another, better day, our time together might bring both of us joy— the bright, apparently endless exchange between us pitching an energetic rightness into everything we touch. Joy so often begins in that, in social life.) And so to write a poem of joy and send it out into the world that includes suffering and injustice and despair and hatred (and joy, and kindness, and beauty, and thought, and love) is potentially not just naïve but careless—an embodied delight turning into active disregard.

But joylessness is at best a temporary answer to despair, and it doesn't make sense to exclude part of what makes lives worth living and protecting—part of what is deprived when the world goes wrong—from our images of the world. The Polish poet Adam Zagajewski famously insists, in Clare Ca-vanagh's translation, that all within earshot "Try to praise the mutilated world." He gets more demanding next time: "You must praise the mutilated world," he instructs, substituting "must" for "try." (It keeps shifting as it goes: "You should" comes next and then yields, near the poem's conclusion, to a straightforward command: "Praise the mutilated world.")

The heightened imperative ("must") comes not in the face of pleasure—"Remember June's long days, / and wild straw-berries, drops of rosé wine."—but after the bleak image that comes after that: "The nettles that methodically overgrow / the abandoned homesteads of exiles." But in calling for praise,

Zagajewski has hedged the poem—its own moments of praise are part of its instruction to others, a rhetorical move that reinforces the very difficulty of doing what it instructs, a small reminder that praise still stands, even amid the poem's persuasive conjuring of the praiseworthy, at one remove.

Appropriately enough, given the subject of this book, I started thinking about joy and poetry in a social setting, talking over drinks with my friend Gabrielle Calvocoressi about joy in poetry and, in particular, in Ross Gay's long poem "Catalog of Unabashed Gratitude." Gaby had already been thinking about it, occasioned in part by her friendship with Gay, and not too much later she wrote a poem of joy of her own, "Praise House: The New Economy," which is, it says, "after and for Ross Gay."

Though neither poem shows any particular connection to Zagajewski's, and though both are far more exuberant than his almost stately progression from instruction through example and back, they overlap with "Try To Praise the Mutilated World" in enough ways to suggest something about the impulses that might govern anyone who accepts Zagajewski's imperative as a call to poetry. Most strikingly, for my purposes here, all three move, in one way or another, into a kind of social setting. Not coincidentally, I think, Zagajewski, whose poem is not at all joyful, creates the most impersonal of these—he lectures; he instructs—though there's a strange intimacy to the way in which amid such instruction he seems almost to be implanting memories in the minds of his readers, memories that verge, often, on surprising particularity. That intimacy is especially pronounced in the poem's one use of "we"—"Remember those moments when we were together"—as if togetherness is another memory being offered to us as readers, who up to and after that point have seemed to be the "you."

Those memories seem, for the most part, humble. The yachts and ships are ones "you" merely watched; the strawberries grow wild; the wine comes in drops; the acorns were there to be gathered freely in the park. It resists separation and elevation, so when "the leaves eddied over the earth's scars" it seems to be a kind of modest healing for us as well, since we are not so far removed from the worst of it, even in our pleasures, in which we do not ask or take too much. In which we are innocent of the mutilation we must now praise.

Gay's "Catalog of Unabashed Gratitude" is far more social—far more interested in enacting a relationship among equals, however one-sided such relationships, in poems, must always be. Its first word is a direct address, "Friends," and it goes out of its way to engage its readers as individuals who must be attended to, going so far at one point as to imagine a literal room for us to rest in as he goes, unabashedly, on:

> And thank *you*, too. And thanks
> for the corduroy couch I have put you on.
> Put your feet up. Here's a light blanket,
> a pillow, dear one,
> for I can feel this is going to be long.
> I can't stop
> my gratitude, which includes, dear reader,
> you, for staying here with me,
> for moving your lips just so as I speak.
> Here is a cup of tea. I have spooned honey into it.

Alongside the slight formality of the address, which reads like an acknowledgment that the room is a poem with no actual couch, blanket, honey or tea, there is the poem's own insistent modesty, in both its diction and its materials—the corduroy couch out of fashion and so presumably old, maybe second-hand, and the tea and honey as apparently natural as Zagajewski's wild strawberries and acorns, and even the wine, which like Gay's tea is processed in accordance with ancient traditions and from a single plant species that brings with it a taste of its earth.

Such modesty makes expressions of joy in poems safer; it diminishes the joy's entanglement with the world's crushing machinery. But that's not to accuse either poem of dishonesty. (The same goes for Calvocoressi's, which is just as studiously humble in its sources of joy.) Gay is a passionate gardener, a man who commits much of his non-literary and academic life to tending the soil and encouraging its fruits. Rather, I find it interesting as a kind of decorum, an awareness of others as both context and individual (even if that individualism is necessarily collective) that guides the work of the poem in a way that's analogous to our awareness of others in our social lives.

It's also, I think, a kind of moral decision, not that far removed from the choices many make about where to shop, what to buy, what to refuse, and what to give away. Gay's exuberance seems to pour into the poem's social awareness, both its constant apologies for taking up so much of our time and its attempts to rub some of the sheen off its materials: The dream bird has "*shabby* wings"; it calls him to strike up the "*rusty* brass band of joy"; the basketball game happens on a "*cockeyed* court"; "love bursts like a throng of *roadside* goldenrod"; etc. He openly exults in everything ramshackle, jerry-rigged, broken down and still at work:

> and thank you, too, this knuckleheaded heart, this
>   pelican heart,
> this gap-toothed heart flinging open its gaudy maw
> to the sky, oh clumsy, oh bumblefucked,
> oh giddy, oh dumbstruck,
> oh rickshaw

All of these moves seem playful, a more-than-winking acknowledgment of its artifice that serves as its own kind of welcome, as permission to put aside, for now, whatever in us might otherwise object that this is not the whole story of the world. Reading it, I feel the way I often do with an old friend—or

that rare new friend in whom everything already feels familiar—
free to follow the joke past reality or precision because we both
already know what we're up to and who we are, and because our
time together brings joy, which colors everything.

But unlike that moment in the friendship, these poems do
carry some greater obligation to test their joy against despair
or injustice—to make themselves answerable and available
to the mutilated world. At one point, the impulse towards
humility carries all the way into gratitude for the harm not
done, offering thanks to the ancestor:

> who loved you
> before she knew you by not slaughtering
> the land; thank you
> who did not bulldoze the ancient grove
> of dates and olives,
> who sailed his keys into the ocean
> and walked softly home; who did not fire, who did not
> plunge the head into the toilet, who said *stop*,
> *don't do that....*

The run of negations is shadowed by the harm that often,
elsewhere, simultaneously, *is* done. Those moments take up only
small patches of the poem, but they do come up. In the poem's
riskiest (risky, that is, to its wish for our assent) and perhaps most
essential move, Gay's exuberance slams into destruction and goes
on without pause, its anaphora another form of exuberance:

> And thank you the baggie of dreadlocks I found in a
>   drawer
> while washing and folding the clothes of our murdered
>   friend;
> the photo in which his arm slung
> around the sign to "the trail of silences"; thank you
> the way before he died he held

his hands open to us; for coming back
in a waft of incense or in the shape of a boy
in another city looking
from between his mother's legs,
or disappearing into the stacks after brushing by;
for moseying back in dreams where,
seeing us lost and scared
he put his hand on our shoulders
and pointed us to the temple across town.

It likely matters here that Gay points toward the murder
of someone he knew, rather than injustices that never touched
his life, much as it likely matters, especially given how little the
poem touches on systemic oppression and the like, that Gay is
black—that we as readers can safely assume he knows about
such things, since injustice in America has so many ways of entering black lives. But part of the point here is the ability to
talk over devastation and horror, to name it persuasively in the
voice of joy, much as W.S. Merwin does in another extraordinary
poem of gratitude, "Thanks," which concludes:

with the animals dying around us
taking our feelings we are saying thank you
with the forests falling faster than the minutes
of our lives we are saying thank you
with the words going out like cells of a brain
with the cities growing over us
we are saying thank you faster and faster
with nobody listening we are saying thank you
thank you we are saying and waving
dark though it is

Unlike Gay, Merwin gives the last word to the darkness he
conjures. "Catalog of Unabashed Gratitude" concludes in a more
social and more joyful stance, its last bit of bad news more of a

call to joy than something to resist, its final line maybe a little too neat, the extra rhyme maybe a little too flat, but that feels almost irrelevant, given how astonishing, how surprisingly personal, the line before it feels, and how generative the last and largest bad news becomes in the almost slapstick final stanza here:

> Soon it will be over,
>
> which is precisely what the child in my dream said,
> holding my hand, pointing at the roiling sea and the sky
> hurtling our way like so many buffalo,
> who said *it's much worse than we think*,
> *and sooner*, to whom I said
> *no duh child in my dreams*, what do you think
> this singing and shuddering is,
> what this screaming and reaching and dancing
> and crying is, other than loving
> what every second goes away?
> Goodbye, I mean to say.
> And thank you. Every day.

It's not a coincidence, though, that both poems, like Zagajewski's and Calvocoressi's, are, as Gay's title makes explicit, catalogues. Or that, unlike "Praise the Mutilated World," which is a call to praise but not actually joyous, all three move with remarkable speed, so much so that the poems felt awareness of their materials as distinctive beings may be among their most impressive achievements. (Merwin's "Thanks" seems most willing to elide such differences, reaching instead toward something almost universal, an encompassing and adamant "we.") Amid their humility, they make a case for abundance, too.

In taking up Gay's summons, Calvocoressi makes cataloging even more integral to the style and syntax of her poem. "Praise House" is almost thirty lines in before its first complete sentence, and even there the subject and verb ("I want") merely point to the next marvel. Or, they almost only do so. If Merwin's poem goes almost as far toward universality as one plausibly could and still praise, Calvocoressi's is strikingly personal—and personal in a way that is also inevitably (and consciously) political. When Gaby and I sat down for that drink ("One cold beer / before I drink it and get sick," she writes in "Praise House"; that evening, she didn't finish the beer.) and as we talked about "Catalog of Unabashed Gratitude," she was already asking how many truly joyful poems were written by women. We didn't come up with many.

When that first subject and verb takes the reins, no longer tucked inside some sort of subordinate clause, she has just written about two guys: "Bros, yes"—the "yes" one of the countless doors and windows Calvocoressi opens so that our doubt can escort in the usually unlaudable, the sometimes-downright-awful. "But lovely / in the golden light with brims swung / to the back." "I want," she continues, "shoulders like / they have. Want my waist to taper / to an ass built like the David's." That "want," that movement toward masculinity, moves in all kinds of directions, one of them queer. And if queerness in a poem is no longer unusual, a queer body still has radical meaning in our society, especially when it crosses traditional barriers between male and female. (As I write this, the state of North Carolina, where both Gaby and I live, has just passed a bill of sweeping cruelty, one it escorted in under the cover of easily manufactured panic about a law in Charlotte that guaranteed trans people the right to use the bathroom for their gender.)

That Calvocoressi, in that same movement, expresses dissatisfaction with her body, that her insufficient body is still the vehicle of praise—that so much of what it praises is attached to or enters that body, felt things: taste, touch, smell—suggests both humility (her materials, for the most part, just as humble as Gay's) and a faintly Whitmanesque willingness to stand at the center of a universe, though in this case it stands there eccentrically, by choice. If poems *are* social, part of their social lives in a culture that is at once diverse and discriminatory must be, like the rest of our social lives, alert to difference that is ultimately experienced and expressed at the level of the individual, the point where social forces intersect and are altered by difference that is never categorical in experience or whole.

But why these catalogs? Why these many multiples, this bounty? Joy, in our lives off the page, often seems to spring from just one thing—a new love, good news, time with friends, the lifting of a long despair. If you and I ever do meet for dinner and I happen to be feeling joyful that evening and you ask me why, there's a good chance that I'll describe a single cause. I will not tell you to look at the color of the light outside and smell the air, and—see that person over there, how he holds his fork? But if I try to imagine a joyous poem with just one subject, it doesn't seem joyous at all. Joy is, I think, a kind of pull, a sense of appetite and invitation—the sensation beginning, or so it feels, beyond the body, pouring in. It's a belief about the world—however brief—that feels almost objective. A feeling of radiant health, harmonized, and if it cannot encompass or at least overlook whatever we see, it falters. It's an all-or-nothing state. And the joyful poem has to bring us inside—or leave us out.

"Praise House" seems especially invested in that encompassing abundance. Whereas "Catalog of Unabashed Gratitude" will often spend an entire stanza on a single source of joy, Calvocoressi's poem rarely gives more than two consecutive sentence fragments to any one thing—and those fragments, with their nouns in charge, lend a sense that the things of the world are lining up to be noticed. Across those fragments, "Praise House" shifts frequently from personal experience to the experiences of others overseas to details of the world at large. And something in that feels generous. It feels eager to share, not just in the colloquial sense of telling others what you think or feel, but in a way that is sturdier and stranger: "The New Economy," the subtitle says, a phrase the poem seems, really, to aspire to. It's an economy based on naming, on welcoming, and it does not refuse our getting and spending, nor does it suggest that they always lay waste to our powers. (The shirt, the car, the dumplings, the bow ties, the plane ticket, the "perfect green shirt" that seems to confer worth on the man who wears it—all are purchased, as is so much else.)

"Praise House" does not intend to defer joy until a better world arrives, but it makes explicit that it would favor this world's destruction if that's what it takes. The declaration comes suddenly and out of a seemingly very different stance:

> Mary Oliver. I love her. I really do.
> The baseball she gave me
> that says, "Go Sox!" Though, I love
> the Orioles. Old Bay on all my shrimp.
> And justice. And cities burning
> if people need to burn them to get free.

There's a kind of logic that runs from the declaration of love for Mary Oliver, a poet that many of Calvocoressi's friends likely scorn, through so much that is marketed and cherished, both—the baseball given, the teams adored, and the beloved brand of seasoning with its willfully antiquated name—through the abstract concept into praise for the concrete, particular destruction of things as essential as shelter if those in need need that. I'm not sure how often the burning of a city, however inevitable once giving up has started to seem like the only alternative, has ever made people free, but I'm also not sure that's the point. The new economy the poem seeks to enact is one that allows all to live in abundance, in joy, in terms that are meaningful to them and accommodating of the joy of others, too. It's a place where everyone can move freely and askance.

"Praise House" includes one of the best sex scenes I've ever read in a poem, one Calvocoressi seems, when we finally get

there, to have been building toward all along. Early on, there's
the shift from a decaying peach to her partner's still-ripe flesh:

> How peaches mold into compost in a single day:
> orange to gray to darkness into dirt.
> Her ankle's taste. The skin
> right under the knob, delicate
> as a tomatillo's shroud.

Then there's the admission that she wants a torso like
the bros have, which concludes "I admit it: / this body's not
enough for me. / Still I love it." And after that the first mention of bow ties, with their implication of cross dressing, and
then, a little later, more intimate:

> Boxer briefs and packing socks
> in jockey shorts. Strap ons.
> Soft and hard. Welcome in her hand
> and in mine as I greet the real me.

That "real me." That welcome. And then, at last, as soon
as she has mentioned the cities burning, the poem races toward its end:

> My grandmother gardening
> in the late light. Sun Ra. The first time.
> Paris, even though I've never been
> there. Natal plums. Tattoos everlasting:
> Clouds. Orion's belt. Pushing inside her
> with both hands holding myself
> up. My weight. Her grabbing and saying,
> "God." "Fuck." The neighbors.
> Casablanca. Not knowing anything.
> Angels. Mashed potatoes. Good red wine.

"'God.' 'Fuck.' The neighbors." I love how it spins back
out, maybe suggesting a sudden realization that the neighbors can hear, maybe just thinking of someone else to be
grateful for. If the last line doesn't quite do it here, either,
that, too, seems a little beside the point. Not after that ex-
quisitely broken, percussive collection of fragments in which
you can almost feel how a body encounters itself in awareness of another, both lifting up and pressing down, "Pushing
inside her / with both hands holding myself / up. My weight.
Her grabbing and saying, / 'God.' 'Fuck.'"

Gay's poem has sex (pun intended, I guess), too. At first,
as in "Praise House," he seems to be with a specific partner,
the other half of the "we," before explicitly turning back to
the reader:

> The room in my mind with the blinds drawn
> where we nearly injure each other
> crawling into the shawl of the other's body.
> Thank you say it plain:
> fuck each other dumb.

One of the obvious differences between a poem and a social
occasion is what it sanctions. In writing, we can tell strangers
things that would likely be too intimate for an in-person
encounter. But Gay pushes past that sanction as he returns
to the reader, mocking his own excitement in a metaphor that
should be out of bounds:

> And you, again, you, for the true kindness
> it has been for you to remain awake
> with me like this, nodding time to time
> and making that noise which I take to mean
> *yes*, or, *I understand*, or, *please go on*
> *but not too long*, or, *why are you spitting*
> *so much*, or, *easy Tiger*

> *hands to yourself.* I am excitable.
> I am sorry. I am grateful.
> I just want us to be friends now, forever.
> Take this bowl of blackberries from the garden.
> The sun has made them warm.
> I picked them just for you. I promise
> I will try to stay on my side of the couch.

I admit to struggling with that stanza. As a big, furry, overweight, straight guy who doesn't really have to worry about advances from men *or* women, I don't feel threatened or diminished, but at the same time, I'm aware that when a poem addresses me it's asking me to stand in the same place as any other potential "you" who might pick it up, and I feel in some way accountable for the space I share with them. If Ross Gay and I were two friends hanging out and he made a joke like this, it probably wouldn't bother me. In that context, it would, I think, be clear that neither of us thought it was ever OK to touch someone who doesn't want to be touched, that merely "trying" to stay away is absurd, but here, reading this poem, I don't feel entirely, or exclusively, myself, and I'm not sure how to react—I'm not sure what to feel, how the someone else I might be standing with might feel.

≈

> My mother's seizures—specifically
> that I don't have them.
> That I can answer Ross' call
> or not because we live Harmonious
> and are always talking somehow.
> Tapestries with their gluttony of deer.

As in "Catalog," the praise reaches out to the harm not done, the suffering not felt. It also encompasses the person not there—which happens to be Gay himself. To state the obvious, real people matter to the things we write and read, and the audience of a poem is usually only partly real, aspired to, uncertain, an extrapolation from the people we've actually met and the things they like and value and are moved by. We "are always talking somehow," Calvocoressi writes, and her poem itself is evidence of that, even as it does not address him or anyone.

I write, in part, because writing's only *like* conversation. You get to slow down and think it through, try again, look it up, try to get it right. You get to wait until you have something to say and think about how someone else might respond to it. You get to try to find some place where different people whose opinions matter to you might overlap and aim for that narrow eye in the Venn diagram they unwittingly compose. Or, I do. And some others do too, but not all of them are you, and not all of you are them. But it still gets us back to real people at some point. And it still matters, to the value of the poem and to the potential of the language and to the meaning of life itself, how we think about them. And sometimes it just matters immensely—matters, among other things, to our ability to step away from them long enough to write—that we know that they are still dependably there.

Is joy in a poem really that different from joy somewhere else? Joy is spontaneous, of course, and poems, for the most part, are not. And a joyful poem, as opposed to the joy we experience in our own bodies first, has more work to do to prove itself proper to the mutilated world: Poems, being somewhat unreal, have to earn their way into the world in a way that people do not. But poems are real, too, and answerable to reality; they exist because people need or want them— want to make them and sometimes want to read them, too. And in their reality, which is part of their achievement—their having *become*, like Pinocchio, real—they also become instructive, a lesson about how things might work. I don't think it's a coincidence that both the poems I'm writing about in this section exhibit their greatest power before they conclude. Joy doesn't really add up. It is, by definition, exceptional. It is a ripeness, the fruit almost more full than its skin can allow: I am bursting with joy, we say. It's sometimes a bit of a mess.

The biggest difference, I think, is that the joy in a poem must be shared to exist. Joy, unlike many of the things that attract us to others, can be an individual experience. Beauty is in the eye of the beholder; kindness must be put into action; humor intends to make someone laugh. But joy, unlike poems, needs no audience. And so a joyful poem—a successful one, at least—is likely to be more generous, more social, more invested in others, than the experience of joy itself. And that generosity, paradoxically, seems to point us, at least in our present tense, away from sharing anything that costs a lot. "Tapestries," Calvocoressi writes, "with their gluttony of deer." They are among the only expensive things in either poem, but it's a public expense. We go to see them in public spaces these days. And how public both poems seem. How eager to make us—to make "us"—at home.

❦

But poems are also for show. Their most social gestures, the ones that seem to enact a conversation with a reader, are often their least spontaneous—as with Gay offering all of us a seat on the couch. And so to talk about a social virtue in a poem is not to talk about its rhetoric as virtuous but rather to ask how it makes the things we value in other spaces available in this act and object of sequential privacies—privacies made valuable in part by the knowledge that each other might exist.

In its postures, Paisley Rekdal's "Happiness" is proudly ungenerous. Its opening lines move quickly from defensive to defiant, invoking her readers in a taunt:

> I have been taught never to brag but now
> I cannot help it: I keep
> a beautiful garden, all abundance,
> indiscriminate, pulling itself
> from the stubborn earth: does it offend you
> to watch me working in it,
> touching my hands to the greening tips or
> tearing the yellow stalks back, so wild
> the living and the dead both
> snap off in my hands?

I'm pretty thin-skinned. If someone in real life asked me "does it offend you" I'd be at best uncomfortable. But here it thrills me, because I'm the speaker at least as much as I am the person being spoken to, because I am, here, a little bit unreal. From the initial protestation of helplessness (Gay's poem starts that way, too) it grows powerful, apparently free from what either neighbor or reader might think. "Does it offend you?" she asks, and then gives us line after line of detailed description, making sure we see as clearly as possible that which might offend. It's almost lewd.

Rekdal calls the poem "Happiness" in part, I suspect, because "happy" has baggage. To be happy, etymologically, is to be fortunate, in a way that, at least for now, her neighbors—one with "stuttering / fingers," the other a "broken / love"—are not. She seems to want us to notice that she's behaving badly, just as she does at the outset when she tells us she knows better than to brag—then brags.

The second time she asks the question, we're no longer posed against her. "Does it offend *them*," she asks this time, meaning the neighbors who come to her seeking solace. And in that moment the poem becomes more personal. The "you" that was maybe us was generic. Now she's talking about specific people and their individualized despair. She's talking about the need she turns away. You could make a case that this poem is a warning about self-absorption, about self-indulgence. Consider the poem's final lines:

> I want to take my neighbors into the garden
> and show them: Here is consolation.
> Here is your pity. Look how much seed it drops
> around the sparrows as they fight.
> It lives alongside their misery.
> It glows each evening with a violent light.

"Here is your pity" sounds brutal. It's the kind of line that, when someone says it in a movie, accompanies something hitting someone in the face or the gut or the crotch. And "violent light" is every bit as worrying as it is enticing—it makes me think of the gorgeous sunsets air pollution smears across the sky. But the line before it makes it hard for me to imagine this poem is something as small as a warning: "It lives alongside their misery." That, of course, is what neighbors do: They live alongside. I think the poem is trying to embrace that, to be honest about that, to foreground the violence of our ardent embrace of the world—"so wild / the living and the dead both / snap off in my hands"; "silent as a point of bone"; "like a stream of kerosene being lit"— as well as the ways we can grow blind to others in it—and the ways that our fear of such blindness can niggle, inflect, distract: "is it / indiscriminate?" she asks, referring to her garden but clearly meaning more than that, as well. Meaning abundance. Bounty. Something like joy.

The speaker is, at times, defensive, but not enough to stop. The poem is a rationalization, but it rests its case on beauty, and the poem's beauty makes it hard for me to withhold my assent. At one moment she protests, "It is such a small thing / to be proud of, a garden." I love how the antecedent of "it" comes in belatedly, as if she were trying to slip it in under the cover of plainness. It's a very different version of the smallness that runs through "Catalog of Unabashed Gratitude" and "Praise House," where smallness is integral to the experience, where it's one of the sources of joy—that it doesn't take too much. Here it plays as an excuse, one she repeats soon thereafter, more literally, after a different excuse that feels instead too large ("Should I, too, not be loved?"): "It is only a little time, a little space."

"Happiness" isn't joyful. The tone of the poem slides from stately to restrained, holding back the boundlessness of joy and the encroach of despair, which also blooms. Densities of sound pile up against its caution—life: insistent and astonishing, rampant, indiscriminate, bounteous. But I do feel joy reading it. Its dark vitality, the same dark vitality the speaker tries to restrain, fills me. And it does so, to a large extent, on the same ground on which "Catalog" and "Praise House" do. "Happiness," though, is far more performative than either of those. That's not to say that Gay and Calvocoressi aren't performing, too; it's just that their performances seem to line up with them, embodying in the characters of Ross and Gabrielle a bearing on life that the actual Ross and Gaby, somewhere on the other side of the poems and time, seem to have meant.

In "Happiness," I don't feel safe assuming that the speaker is a version of Rekdal. The poem's intelligence seems to move at a different angle than the speaker's, and that divergence, combined with the poem's own achievement of reality, makes the speaker's role more habitable. The paradoxical combination of reality and unreality—the sense that I am not displacing a real person, Rekdal, by stepping into the speaker's role—proves permissive. I can touch the world, in its terrible, abundant beauty, and I can walk away, having felt myself full of such perilous vitality, having done no actual harm.

And this, too, is part of the social life of art—its enabling of others. It's odd, how uniformly negative that word's connotations are for us. Whatever is enabled is, by implication, destructive, as in our entrenched vocabulary of addiction. But it's worth noting the obvious—that there are things art cannot do. That a poem only touches us metaphorically: Even as it moves me my body goes nowhere. It destroys nothing more than a piece of paper. It creates, in reality, only itself. Sometimes, I think, we talk about poetry as if that weren't the case, and our imagination of what a poem can ethically accomplish narrows as a result.

The virtue of a poem may be, in some cases, that it gives us a chance to do or feel what elsewhere we shouldn't. But even then, poems are part of the same social existence whose rules it manifests at odd angles. My Facebook feed regularly shows me the power of poems to wound, to offend—shows me people wounded and angered by poems they have read. And so part of these performances becomes, as well, their audible awareness of their potential audiences: how they allow us to enter these alternate worlds in confidence that we are not endorsing harm and will not be subject to the kinds of harm that we regard as unjust. That's not always a good thing, by any means, and we don't always handle it well. But it's part of the path poems cut through a world in which poetry is—thank god—almost never the most important thing, and where a poem's ability to incorporate the things that matter more (life, death, love, injustice, joy, the mutilation of the world) is the very source of its value.

☙

Alan Shapiro's "Thanks for Nothing" responds, like "Praise House," to "Catalog of Unabashed Gratitude," though it seems, at first, to be turning "Catalog" on its head. Its title's a play on the familiar sarcastic phrase, and its opening stanza lands in bitter sarcasm, too:

> Thank you, I don't know
> who, or what,
> for nothing
> I can know

> which something
> once was spit from
> for no reason
> but to be
> sucked back
> to nothing so that
> nothing could feel
> what?—its nothingness
> more keenly?

I should probably note that Alan (he was my first mentor and remains an important friend, and he let me publish the poem in *At Length*) is friends with Gaby and Ross Gay, and that he appears, though he isn't named, in "Catalog." He was the "61-year-old" on the aforementioned "cockeyed court"

> on which in a half-court 3 v 3 we oldheads
> made of some runny-nosed kids
> a shambles, and the 61-year-old
> after flipping a reverse lay-up off a back door cut
> from my no-look pass to seal the game
> ripped off his shirt and threw punches at the gods
> and hollered at the kids to admire the pacemaker's scar
> grinning across his chest

That, for anyone who knows Alan, is a pretty good example of the route (at least in his social life) he takes toward joy. He's a brilliant and relentless comic of despair, one for whom the sources of despair, in giving occasions for humor, become sources of social vitality—sources, even, of joy. And so it turns out, soon enough, that Shapiro's not kidding about "Thanks" here—or, at least, not entirely. The gratitude is also real.

For Shapiro to praise the mutilated world, it's not so much a question of managing our complicity in its mutilation as it is of standing inside the scale of cosmic indifference to all joy and all suffering (an indifference that is for some a source of even more suffering), one that excuses any joy we can wring from it but is no more an excuse than the small-ness Calvocoressi and Gay shelter in. It also turns out to be a source of joy itself—the very vastness of the universe a gift, however darkly and disastrously given.

The poem moves, headlong and wobbly, from the cosmic as far down as the microbial, as far down as the individual, the personal, the interpersonal, "this last, this / best love." And the poem grows joyful, the deep pleasure of writing, of being in motion, in language, agile and alert, even in view of his pending oblivion, even as it encompasses the paltriness of its own means and motivations:

> Thanks, truly,
> for so little.
> For the shifty
> ever busy solace
> behind the tortured
> logic that would link
> loss to beauty,
> nectar to sorest need,
> the clever ruses
> we devise
> to make of so little
> given something
> larger than it is.

That "truly" is hard to pin down, maybe a little sarcas-tic, maybe an example of the tricks we try to play on each other and ourselves to make life in the shadow of extinction bearable. But like most of those tricks, also sincere. It's the first moment in the poem when I sense an awareness of au-dience—outside, that is, the implication of audience in the poem's restless work to give pleasure. Until that point, rhetorically, Shapiro has directed his address to the unknowable, unnamable, and in fact unaddressable source of being and nonbeing alike. That imaginary auditor is so indifferent to him that, when he writes of "you" as "I don't know / who, or what," even that implied question of its nature is purely rhetorical and palpably insincere. Meanwhile, the poem assumes our consent, sweeping us up in first-person plural that, contra "you," involves everyone who lives and dies.

"Truly," though, feels like a negotiation of sorts, an encounter with something caring enough to believe or disbelieve what he says. It's still part of the show, of course—the whole poem is a master performance—but it's enough of a wobble to remind me that this poem, like "Happiness," is in part about and thoroughly indebted to our social lives but does not aspire to encounter us, the potential readers, as social beings, and will not entangle itself in the decorums that "Catalog" and "Praise House" engage.

Less social, more of a show with the familiar fourth wall in place, "Thanks for Nothing," like "Happiness," feels more like a single ongoing speech. It's not a catalog, not really— or if it is, it amounts to a pretty short catalog and a rather long poem. Its sources of joy feel increasingly singular, and personal—and finally private, so that one of its pleasures is its refusal of social conventions. When Shapiro gets to sex, it feels more illicit than Calvocoressi's sex scene does. The lover's body is more on display, though still covered—maybe because it's covered—and her desire has moved out of the bedroom and into a public space, where it is less sanctioned and more secretive for being at risk of being seen:

> last week
> at the opening,
> in the hall
> with people milling
> all around her,
> cup of wine

in one hand, how she
somehow caught
my eye so I alone
would see her slyly
slip her free hand
down her pants
and out and
nonchalantly brush
her fingertips
across her nose
to breathe in
her own bouquet,
her pleasure
in herself so
nearly animal,
her pleasure
in my seeing it
so not

Those two simultaneous pleasures, the "animal" converted into something social (but scandalously so, privately so) and yet maintaining its "animal" nature, too. How different it would be to have stood in the gallery and noticed it going on, not so much because seeing is different than hearing but because here, in the poem, it's being shared—the privacy of it made public and yet staying private, too, because a poem keeps its posture even as it heads into the world.

Joy is an oddly binary emotion. You're never a little bit joyful, and it's hard to imagine feeling a partial joy, one that didn't touch whatever else you're feeling. All is joy, or nothing is—which means that joy, like art, deceives. Like art it stands inside and outside the world at once, contingent on experience that is itself contingent on the means by which experience is converted—on art. It's absolute and imprecise—untrue and actual.

Shapiro presses the poem into what seems most funda-mental, most real—our ultimate unreality and our massive, boundless nonexistence, which is our only real contact with infinity. And the joy of the poem overwhelms that, too, in much the same way Dickinson described the brain as being "wider than the Sky." At times, nothingness becomes a kind of fuel for the poem, as in his earlier poem "Joy" the worst of it, evaded, even if only for a moment, turns into vitality, the herd of antelopes running from the lion

                        swerving as one,
        their leaping strides now
                        leaping higher,
                                faster,
        even after,
                it seems,
                        the fear subsides—
        after the fear and
                        the relief
                                they keep
        on running
                for nothing but
                        the joy of running,
        though
                it could be
                        any one of them
        is running
                from its fallen
                        mother or father,
        sister or brother,
                across the wide
                                savanna,
        under a bright sun
                        into fresher grass.

In that poem, as in "Gratitude for Nothing," Shapiro lands on a reminder of the underlying darkness, but it also feels to me like the poem is still running even then, and that running is still joyous, whatever started it and wherever it leads. The description of nothingness at the end of "Gratitude" is full, still spilling over, still delighted in turning over its own fig-ures, still, even in its final lines, inflected with the dark humor that makes even the most alienating knowledge into some-thing with social power:

> Which means, I think,
> it's you I'm picturing,
> you I'm longing for
> and running from,
> blind giver and dumb taker,
> my stone deaf end
> and origin, whom
> I pretend
> hears me pretend
> to thank for being
> both somehow
> (I don't know how)
> the dangled carrot
> tempting me forward
> into nothing and the stick
> of nothing
> nothing beats me with.

He's pretending, he says—both that nothingness can hear him and that he's grateful for the nothing that, in reality, can't hear. While it's tempting to play with the idea that if he's only pretending that nothing can hear then he is, Polyphemus-like, actually saying that something can, that feels like a stretch. I'm more convinced that pretending is its own potential source of reality. It's what allows the social life of the poem here to come into being, not because it lets us hide from each other the reality of our pending, eternal irrelevance, but because it allows us to sing and be sung to, to make nothing into something, not so much *ex nihilo* as in its participation in the ongoingness of language, joking, beauty (and, yes, despair) here in a place where making something is a source of joy and being in the audience for that made thing is a source of joy, a chance to marvel at all that humans can do, even as what we're doing is telling each other that we can't do enough.

The social life of poetry is strange. "Poetry makes nothing happen," Auden wrote. And then, less famously, but more interesting, he went on:

> it survives
> In the valley of its making where executives
> Would never want to tamper, flows on south
> From ranches of isolation and the busy griefs,
> Raw towns that we believe and die in; it survives,
> A way of happening, a mouth.

That poetry will presumably go on outliving us for a very long time doesn't give me much solace, but these lines, claiming that they will, do. "A way of happening, a mouth." Also, an occupation of the present tense, even if it's occupied by a series of images that already feel flecked with nostalgia. Joy is an anti-utopian force, even if it allows us to imagine a better world, because it brings us so wholly into the moment of its being, here in the mutilated world. So, too, for Shapiro's poem, where the mind's delight outruns its materials, even as those materials—that overriding immateriality—are the very surface on which it runs.

I am writing this essay right now in my front yard. My wife is inside grading. You, if you exist, are, as you read this, somewhere else, at some other time, some other "right now." I do not, at the moment, feel joy. I am not, for the most part, a joyful person. But at times, in writing this, I have felt something close to joy, that seamlessness in which the ideas, in coming together, have conjured you, whoever you might be. In reading all of these poems, too, I have felt something like that, myself strangely real, running so fluently in time that time ceases to matter—the burden of my being now a gift, an ease in which the weight of the world registers fully in its being so easy to lift. In "Thanks for Nothing," I can feel Shapiro feeling that, the long present tense of writing the poem becoming a single moment in the world, of the world, but also absolved for the time of our insufficiency in it.

One of the deepest gifts of our social life is our ability to confer that kind of reality on each other, the ways in which the currents of our sharing make "the real me," as Calvocoressi puts it, someone we can meet in meeting someone else. It isn't true that poetry changes nothing, even in the sense that Auden meant. Human history has plenty of examples of poems becoming a significant political force. But poems are also a way of living fully in this world, the one we wish were better, even of living more fully inside that wish. To do that work, they must be credible: A poem as pure escapism cannot, at least for me, provide a means of escape. "Earth's the right place for love," wrote Frost. "I don't know where it's likely to go better." It's also the right place for joy. And in speaking persuasively enough, ecstatically enough, of the mutilated world, of its amazements, of our being here, poems, like people, might conjure us. They might make us real.

"Who Know in Singing Not to Sing": On Decorum

It's no wonder we've stopped talking about decorum in art. Neither the literary nor the social applications of the term sit well in an age that must, at minimum, give lip service to ideals of democracy, even when undermining democracy itself. *Decorum,* for many of us, suggests a kind of secret handshake. It presents privilege as achievement—as if the habits of the well-off were emblematic of distinction—and walls-off opportunity from those whose different cultural habits therefore suggest some sort of inadequacy. Definitions of the word, whether in literary or cultural contexts, consistently involve words like "propriety" and "polite," neither of which leaves any room for pushing back against, or imagining value independent of, a society in which power continues to aggregate in the hands of an elite that invests first and often and immorally in the underpinnings of its own elite status—even if it now knows enough to be wary of the word ("elite") itself.

And yet I'd like to argue that there's still a role for decorum in a multicultural society—as an awareness of the ways we do and sometimes should rein in some of our impulses as we enter the shared spaces that allow individuals to meet. I'm especially interested in understanding how decorum, as I'm defining it here, might run counter to something more apparently expressive. We say that someone "breaks into song," and the implication is, I think, that singing is unrestrained, unchecked, the voice reaching for a fullness of volume, force and range. Decorum, at least in my imagination of it, is an expectation that we will leave certain things unbroken, at least initially, until we know those around us well enough to know their vulnerabilities—to know what parts of them are easily broken, too.

In treating the impulse to sing, to break into song, as indecorous, I may be relying too heavily on my own experience. I enjoy singing—the feeling of power and freedom, my body becoming a conduit for beauty—but only when I'm on my own. It turns out I'm a truly terrible singer, so much so that friends have politely asked me to stop singing around them. The pleasure depends, for me, on an imagined audience, an unreal audience, one that hears my voice as I hear it in my head.

More broadly, I grew up in a culture in which restraint was a cardinal virtue and self-display suspect. Still, I think that the desire to sing—and the awareness of a variety of reasons singing might be unwelcome or improper—plays an essential role in our contemporary poetry. In the different forms it takes, restraint (especially restraint in accordance with established decorums) can produce an impressively complex embodiment of the ways social awareness—for good and for ill—interacts with individual desire. And I think, too, that in a time when the very forces that control our economy and govern our lives invest so heavily and so effectively in enchanting us, when superlatives wear out from overuse so fast we have to enlist words like "literally" to intensify what we say (the phenomena are not, I think, unrelated), the desire to resist the urge to sing—to chant, to enchant—is likely to pull particularly hard, even as the desire to sing persists and, in some situations, pulls harder, too.

Writing about Berryman's *Dream Songs* in the late 70s, Robert Pinsky claimed, "Berryman's language seems to me to grow first of all from the need for a vocabulary that does not restrict or embarrass him." The essay goes on, "the colloquial words help the syntax, the gags, and the personae in a general effort to admit another kind of phrase—like 'a smothering southern sea'—*just as in ordinary talk* tough-slangy lines such as 'all that jazz' often excuse and qualify a phrase the speaker feels may seem too elevated or pretentious." Those ideas of embarrassment and excuse speak, I think, to a necessary sorrow. Poetry remains an art of decorum, and the particular decorums that inhibit a given poet from full-on full-throatedness (or, in other cases, from restraint) as well as the strategies a given poet uses to make more room for song, score the presence of the particular world in which each self must attune itself in order to be heard.

~

I started thinking about this while I was working on a review of Patricia Lockwood's *Motherland Fatherland Homelandsexuals*, a review that spent a fair amount of time on "Rape Joke." It's a poem that bumps up against two very different sets of expectations, expectations that run counter to each other. Lockwood is a prominent part of a literary culture that values wit and distrusts sentimentality, but she's also part of a culture, the one we're all part of as Americans, that still treats sexual violence as both a taboo topic and, with alarming frequency, an inconsequential act. "Rape Joke" generates much of its energy and genius in trying to navigate, simultaneously, these two very different standards.

The aesthetic conflict of the poem is right there in the title. According to *The New York Times*, Lockwood decided to finish the poem (she'd already written notes for it) after hearing about an appalling crack by a comedian named Daniel Tosh:

> That summer, during a stand-up set, the comedian Daniel Tosh went into an extended riff on rape jokes, which prompted a woman in the audience to shout, "Rape jokes are never funny." Tosh's response — "Wouldn't it be funny if that girl got raped by, like, five guys right now?" — sparked a nationwide debate about taboos in comedy: Are there things we just can't laugh about, and who is the "we" that gets to laugh and in what circumstances?

If a poem is in part about its style, then "Rape Joke" is about all the ways in which it's impossible for a victim to talk about rape—especially if you're a poet, like Lockwood, whose style (which is to say, in part, the way her poems imagine their audience) insists on irreverence. Near the end of the poem, that conflict reaches the surface. Lockwood writes: "The rape joke is that this is finally artless. The rape joke is that you do not write artlessly." Though the poem is in fact remarkably—intricately—artful, it's unlike any other poem Lockwood has published: the events stay recognizably themselves and the narrative elements are realistic. (Just before the conclusion, she writes, "The rape joke is that this is just how it happened.") The use of anaphora, that repeating "The rape joke is," creates, in this case, a sense that the poem is detained, unable to lift off into the jigsaw fancy that marks almost everything else Lockwood writes. It seems to be launching over and again into a wildness it can't quite unlock, as in this passage, where the humor disappears and horror and vulnerability most persistently enter the poem, and where Lockwood keeps turning away, returning twice to the phrase "rape joke" at the end of a paragraph, as if trying to get back to the safety of the conceit:

> The rape joke is that you were facedown. The rape joke is you were wearing a pretty green necklace that your sister had made for you. Later you cut that necklace up. The mattress felt a specific way, and your mouth felt a specific way open against it, as if you were speaking, but you know you were not. As if your mouth were open ten years into the future, reciting a poem called Rape Joke.

> The rape joke is that time is different, becomes more horrible and more habitable, and accommodates your need to go deeper into it.

> Just like the body, which more than a concrete form is a capacity. You know the body of time is *elastic*, can take almost anything you give it, and heals quickly.

The rape joke is that of course there was blood, which in human beings is so close to the surface.

The rape joke is you went home like nothing happened, and laughed about it the next day and the day after that, and when you told people you laughed, and that was the rape joke.

The humor of the poem becomes a conceit for the horror of being raped, not just because we, as readers—because I, as a straight man reading this—become complicit if the poem makes us laugh, but because I can hear the poem she *isn't* writing here, the one that isn't, in her term, "artless." To be raped is to be made powerless; a person's basic freedom to police the perimeters of her body refused; the words of refusal stopped or ignored. It's a terror that is then compounded by our ongoing history of silencing and denying the stories of women and men who have been raped, refusing or stigmatizing the identity that has been forced on each victim. Along with all its other virtues, "Rape Joke" both enacts the difficulty of talking about what has happened and insists on her right to talk about it in the terms she chooses. Stunted and stunning, the poem succeeds not only because its writing is so smart, but also because it seems neither to accept, nor to succeed in erasing, the terms that have been imposed on her. And like any successful poem, it imagines, articulated as the other side of its perimeters, the world in which it hopes however warily to live.

ᴥ

So, too, with Mary Szybist's *Incarnadine*, a rough contemporary of "Rape Joke" and one in which, perhaps not coincidentally, restraint is also most pronounced when Szybist writes in prose. Szybist seems to long for the freedom to live more fully, to sing more wildly, but passion is risky. No matter how well you sing, in some corners of the world—the same corners that still for me look most like a home—singing can make you seem ridiculous. The book's very first poem is called "The Troubadours Etc."; she can hardly finish invoking those medieval singers (the composers of love poems and the models for Ezra Pound's high modernist agenda) before she starts pulling back, diminishing, putting on indifference.

That poem, which feels like one side of an ongoing argument with a romantic partner, is written in a first person plural that refers to her and her husband but that can also feel, to a reader like me, like a wider audience, a contemporary American, educated, middle-class, mostly white culture that mocks whatever diverges from its norms of reason, safety, and skepticism or knowingness. You can hear the language of our time—the style of "our" dismissals—in disparaging lines like "At least they had ideas about love" and "And when we stop we'll follow—what? / Our *hearts*?" And against that there's nostalgia, maybe for the earlier days of their relationship, and certainly for a culture in which such wildness could conceivably be appropriate and, therefore, sustained. She tells her husband: "the troubadours knew how to burn themselves through, / how to make themselves shrines to their own longing. / The spectacular was never behind them." Emphasis, I imagine, on "them."

But as with most things that depend on nostalgia to stand, that bitterness can be a kind of blindness, too. The world in which Szybist, like me, wants to feel at home, even in her un-worldly ecstasies, is a world of at-best only partially earned good fortune and unmistakable privilege. Though there's not much explicitly about race or class or sexuality in *Incarnadine*, they (along with a more explicit awareness of nationalism) lurk in the self-resistance of these poems, as well as their persistent worry about power and self-mocking awareness of her privilege. Even as they hunger for universal meaning, rapturing power, self-forgetful enchantment and childlike innocence, the poems also seem to know how much these ideals imply cultural specifications and entail injustice.

In the prose sequence "Update on Mary," Szybist writes, "When people say 'Mary,' Mary still thinks *Holy Virgin! Holy Heavenly Mother!* But Mary knows she is none of those things." There's something wonderfully childlike about that *"Holy Virgin! Holy Heavenly Mother!"* which suggests both Szybist's sense of herself as fallen and her fear that such associations are childish, along with their continued appeal.

Shifting the author out of the first-person position, like "Rape Joke"—though Szybist refers to herself in third person, rather than second—and sharing something of its repeating structure and rhetorical distancing, "Updates on Mary" allows her to reveal herself in ways that would otherwise seem inappropriate; for example, "Mary secretly thinks she is pretty and therefore deserves to be loved." The flattened prose condescends to the character of herself, adding to the sense of her as childish and naïve, as well as the sense that the adult version of Mary lacks conviction and merely consumes. "At the gym," she writes, mockingly, "Mary watches shows about how she should dress herself, so each morning she tries on several combinations of skirts and heels before retreating to her waterproof boots. This takes a long time, so Mary is busy."

The implication that she's childish (which, in the book's larger movements, is also tied to her frustrated childlessness) turns explicit near the end. Referring to those times when she pretends to read a book but instead "watches the patterns of sunlight through the curtains," Szybist observes, "On those afternoons, she's like a child who has run out of things to think about." The poem ends by enlisting her readers in the challenge of figuring out how to manage her childishness, hoping, it seems, that we can let her off the hook: "The most interesting things to her are clouds. See, she watches them even by moonlight. Tonight, until bedtime, we can let her have those." It's a sad and dispiriting ending, suggesting how much Szybist has to do to let herself engage in a harmless form of pleasure. She must, the poem's form suggests, leave herself, align with those who would judge her (her readers, us, me), forsake the actual experience of watching clouds and leave that to a childish and demeaned version of Mary who will soon have to go to bed. For now, neither version of her will get to sing, neither will break free. And yet lurking in there is the felt awareness of just how little her daydreaming takes in of her surroundings or the society that not only judges it but makes it possible.

The hunger to live in accordance with one's desires cannot be ignored, *Incarnadine* suggests, but neither should the situation of that hunger in a more complex web of realities and illusions. And again, those situations are the photonegative image the poem produces, described in its own deliberate limitations. The poem's decorums—its familiar, to me, forms of restraint, configured in unfamiliar ways—are a form of physical articulation, a partial but surprisingly expansive description of privilege and constraint written into the desire to universalize a certain kind of life—hers, and, by analogy, mine—one in which, as in all lives, the desire, in spite of its implications, is real.

～

On the other side of that hunger for universality stands Claudia Rankine's *Citizen*, a book that works *against* habitual assumptions of universal experience. As with her previous book, this one carries the subtitle *An American Lyric* but is written mostly in a decidedly unlyrical prose—prose that often feels heavy with all the ways it will not, cannot, move. As with *Incarnadine*, it is written in a style that implies and even conjures an audience that is ready to dismiss what it has to say.

Citizen (another rough contemporary) is very much a book about words. It's about words and race and images and bodies and art and horrifying injustice and ordinary injustice and invisibility and assumptions, including assumptions about universality, but it's about these things first and last in being about words, and one word in particular: "you." In a pivotal moment, Rankine writes, in the book's persistent second-person:

> Not long ago you are in a room where someone asks the philosopher Judith Butler what makes language hurtful. You can feel everyone lean in. Our very being exposes us to the address of another, she answers. We suffer from the condition of being addressable.

On the page before that, Rankine tells another story about audiences:

> Someone in the audience asks the man promoting his new book on humor what makes something funny. His answer is what you expect—context. After a pause he adds that if someone said something, like about someone, and you were with your friends you would probably laugh, but if they said it out in public where black people could hear what was said, you might not, probably would not. Only then do you realize you are among "the others out in public" and not among "friends."

Something important and slight happens in the latter passage. For one sentence, the word "you" changes. For that one span, which Rankine renders in paraphrase, allowing it to almost blend into the style of the writing that surrounds it, "you" does not refer to the reader, who everywhere else in the book's prose is being asked to stand in the place of an African American who stands, her or himself, addressable, at the center of a story he or she does not control. For that one sentence, "you" instead refers to an unwittingly, indifferently, closed circle, the audience the comedian assumes—one where everyone is white.

By that point in the book (it crops up on page 48), the habit of hearing "you" as someone black, whatever the reader's actual race, has carved deep enough channels that most will feel the shift, the sudden, startling erasure of the audience member who is addressed as unworthy of address, simultaneously spoken to and unacknowledged, told that she cannot hear. (It's surely no accident that the next page—the Butler story—involves a lecturer saying "our" and "we" in ways that encompass her whole audience.)

Against that background—which, Rankine argues, is the chronic background of black life in America—the meaning of decorum will inevitably be different from the version in *Incarnadine*. Whereas, in Szybist's case, the awareness of others implicated in her restraint often seems in part like a necessary, even healthy, check on a privileged view of the world, in Rankine, it's often a sign of illness:

> When you arrive in your driveway and turn off the car, you remain behind the wheel another ten minutes. You fear the night is being locked in and coded on a cellular level and want time to function as a power wash. Sitting there staring at the closed garage door you are reminded that a friend once told you there exists a medical term—John Henryism—for people exposed to stresses stemming from racism. They achieve themselves to death trying to dodge the build up of erasure. Sherman James, the researcher who came up with the term, claimed the physiological costs were high. You hope by sitting in silence you are bucking the trend.

Much of *Citizen* deals with manifestations of Butler's "addressability," particularly the frequency with which black Americans are addressed in ways that erase their humanity and even announce their nonexistence. The book's second-person address, when placed in front of a white reader, becomes a kind of counter to that—insisting that the reader become addressable, become black, to feel one's whiteness in being assumed to be something else (an inverse of the Zora Neal Hurston quotation she references and then represents in a conceptual art work by Glenn Ligon: "I feel most colored when I am thrown against a sharp white background.") But even as it does this, it continues, for the entirety of its first four sections, to limit itself to a style of writing that seems scored against the possibility of dismissal. It's the kind of writing that studiously avoids—reentering the John Henry-ish task of trying to control the perceptions of those who hardly see you, of erasing yourself to avoid being overlooked—anything that "might make the witness believe that a person is 'insane.'"

That last phrase turns Rankine to Serena Williams. Rankine describes Williams' response, "belatedly," to the bad calls that seem designed to erase her from tennis, a sport in which her blackness is especially visible—and especially threatening. And she goes on to describe the punishment Williams receives, writing:

> Perhaps her punishment was only about context, though context is not meaning. It is a public event being watched in homes across the world. In any case, it is difficult not to think that if Serena lost context in releasing all rules of civility, it could be because her body, trapped in a racial imaginary, trapped in disbelief—code for being black in America—is being governed not by the tennis match she is participating in but by a collapsed relationship that had promised to play by the rules. Perhaps this is how racism feels no matter the context—randomly the rules everyone else gets to play by no longer apply to you and to call this out by calling out "I swear to God!" is to be called insane, crass, crazy. Bad sportsmanship.

The book's first four sections are, I think, orchestrated against all the means by which a black writer, thinker, person, might be accused of breaking the rules. There's a terrible decorum to it that becomes, in its precision, an embodiment of centuries of black voices hiding their bodies, trying to stay one step ahead of the ever-shifting stereotypes used to dismiss, diminish or inflame, disregard, never have even heard, whatever someone black might say. It's part of what makes the book so hard to read—page after page of restraint and control, of avoiding the appearance of rage in the face of outrageous behavior. And even as Rankine's second person address asks me to imagine myself as someone else, as someone not white, my resistance, my anxious self-assertion—my desire to be me—pushes me to remember that I am among those whose presence pushes for that restraint.

Slowly, tentatively, as the book progresses, Rankine experiments with a different relationship to language, with the possibility of play, with the possibility of a *we*, or an *I*, or a *you* that does not erase. But it does so, always, against the weight of that awareness. Here she is in one of the book's earliest moments of lyricism:

> In the darkened moment a body given blue light, a flashlight, enters with levity, with or without assumptions, doubts, with desire, the beating heart, disappointment, with desires—

> Stand where you are.

> You begin to move around in search of the steps it will take before you are thrown back into your own body, back into your own need to be found.

> The destination is illusory. You raise your lids. No one else is seeking.

You exhaust yourself looking into the blue light. All day blue burrows the atmosphere. What doesn't belong with you won't be seen.

You could build a world out of need or you could hold everything black and see. You give back the lack.

You hold everything black. You give yourself back until nothing's left but the dissolving blues of metaphor.

"You hold back the black," Rankine wrote in an earlier version of the poem. "You hold everything black," she writes in the most recent version I have. She tries to do that, too, to go beyond a version of "hold" that means "contain" to something closer to "embrace," but you—I—can feel how difficult it is in the midst of so much holding back. You can feel how much this decorum—this holding back—has kept beyond her reach. For all that *Citizen* attempts a kind of authority over its reader—the power to tell "you" who you are, what you see, hear, say, do, feel, a poetic action at least as old as Shakespeare's Sonnet 73—it can never work altogether free of the weight (a weight that becomes a physical representation) of its awareness of the audience's power to dismiss its claims, its limited power to make another addressable, of the ongoing history of dismissing anything that seems too black.

⤙

Among the many biblical myths of a fall, the Tower of Babel seems especially appealing for some writers today. It's a story of humans being punished for trying to create something that would allow them access to the source of universal truth, and the punishment is the impossibility of speaking to everyone.

We live in a moment when those of us who could previously assume the universality of our experience are being asked, at least in the part of American culture where poetry matters, to think about what such assumptions exclude. We live in a moment when multiculturalism seems to feel like punishment to some—and, just as tellingly, when it feels like a new condition, too.

If contemporary America feels especially fallen to many, if a phrase like "Make America Great Again" resonates for something approaching a plurality of voters, it may be in part (along with and entangled with more naked forms of racism) because the assumption of a universal decorum no longer holds—or, at least, no longer holds as firmly as it did. In a truly multicultural society, a meaningful decorum is likely to be at least somewhat improvisational, based on a complex, intersectional awareness of both the cultural situation in which one person encounters another and the singularity of that other one encounters there. We cannot meet each other without working toward some kind of decorum, some shared if provisional language, but part of that decorum—at least for those of us raised on the assumption that *our* version of decorum was a universal—must, at times, involve some hesitation about our own fluency.

For many, of course, such hesitancy has long (for centuries, in fact) been a default position—because the awareness of others has meant continually navigating assumptions of one's inferiority. In our fallen world—fallen, that is (or intermittently falling, at least) from a potent unreality—decorum remains both part of the problem and, potentially, part of the solution.

To restrain oneself in the face of another is, for better or worse, to recognize the authority of that second person—to grant him or her some say, without speaking, in what gets said or done. To restrain oneself in a poem is, in part, to create the image of an audience and *its* authority. In a world that was always fallen, such images matter, and in a world that is more often and more openly aware of the problems of decorum, decorum becomes especially useful to an art form that embodies, more than most, the complexity of one person trying to reach through shared spaces, shared language, and varying traditions in order to be heard.

In all the poems I've discussed here, abdication adds to the poem's power—it becomes a source of invention, a force defining and harnessing the force that it resists. And in making apparent the risks of lyricism, it renews the boldness of breaking into song in those moments when they do. Something in this makes me wary. It feels too easy to exploit, too easy to turn decorum into another note on the keyboard, a shortcut to success, converting the audience you acknowledge back into a passive player in your aspirations.

But aspiration, is, I think, inevitable, and maybe as essential as inspiration at times. And given that, given that we enter each moment corrupted but, I think, redeemable, maybe even hungry for redemption, (and deserving of it, too, especially if we are willing to take the metaphor into our beings, to exchange our own hopes for others' needs, to give ourselves away), engaging with an audience that may not want to hear from us—for reasons as various as America itself, understandable and awful, individual and cultural, momentary and enduring—permits a deeper engagement with our own experience and all, including all the others, that it entails. In that engagement we might more richly imagine the forces that require deference or allow for respect. We might cultivate a language (our language) that can carry between us more of who we actually are and hope to be, and carry back to us, into us, into our speaking and writing, more of what it means to be reaching out to or refusing an audience with its own claims on the words we use.

"Impersonations of Ordinary": On Humility

1. Elizabeth Bishop

"I caught a tremendous fish." So begins, recognizably but not quite famously, Elizabeth Bishop's "The Fish." Five words, four of which are remarkably plain: "I caught a fish." Minus the one adjective, "tremendous," the only polysyllabic word in the line, it would be so plain that actually saying it would seem like an attempt to ward off talk: "How'd it go?" "I caught a fish."

But "tremendous" is weird: rhythmically, it causes a slight ripple in the meter before the meter has even been established; and the word itself feels a little grand, a little long, ever so slightly out of place, maybe even a little unclear. By the end of the first line, which could be the whole sentence—subject, verb, direct object—all we know about the fish is that it was "tremendous," a claim she, uncharacteristically, leaves unsupported and undefined. The word wavers, holding a place in the poem open, something more or other than the typical fish story's boast, admiring, but uneasy too.

The second line doesn't provide any information about the fish. It does, however, level things out a bit: "and held him beside the boat." The sentence stretches out a little, and with the sense that there's more to the story, the strangeness of that first line, in isolation, starts to fade. There's nothing here to disrupt what James Merrill referred to, writing about Bishop's life, as her "instinctive, modest, lifelong impersonations of an ordinary woman." The only thing potentially out of place is her claim that she held him "beside the boat," rather than in it. But that's not that unusual—not if she only held him there a little while.

Nor is it strange—not yet—that she held him "half out of water" as she says in the third line. But that phrase, with its unblemished literal-mindedness, turns out to be an important symbolic moment in a poem that works very hard to resist turning anything, even the thrice-repeated "rainbow," into a symbol. For almost all of the poem that remains—another 71 lines; another 14 sentences—she tries to keep it there, "half out of water" and half in. I'm tempted to say that she tries to keep it all the way out of the water and all the way in. But that's not quite right. She knows better than that, and knowing better is essential to the self-portrait-in-observation that is at the hesitant, elegant heart of so much of Bishop's work.

～

Etymologically, the word "humility" points earthward. There's a sense of knowing one's place, of never standing up so straight that it would be easy to knock you over. There's a sense of staying on the ground. In that most literal sense (but only in that most literal sense), the word has no application for this unearthly fish hovering in water and air—"the terrible air" where the half of it with gills likely hangs.

The fish fascinates Bishop. The poem seems to exist because she can neither remove the fish from memory nor explain in concrete terms why it persists. She can neither pull it out into the air nor return it to its foreign element. After that first sentence, she comes up short, literally; the next sentence can't even fill a three-beat line, and she waits a line to start again:

> He didn't fight.
> He hadn't fought at all.
> He hung a grunting weight,
> battered and venerable
> and homely.

There's a hint of admiration here, too. It seems related to that lingering word, "tremendous"—that which, at its root, causes one to tremble; that which makes one, in awe, distinct from that which inspires awe. This is the first description of the fish besides "tremendous," and so the first possible explanation for that descriptor. Only "venerable" seems to point in that same direction, but even that stops well short, more still. "Tremendous," for Bishop, seems to be that which manages to endure beneath our notice—something so plain it becomes potentially profound.

Humility, of course, can turn inside out. It can turn into a source of pride. It can also be a hiding place, something like what one becomes or where one goes when afraid to be entirely alive. It's remarkable to watch how hard Bishop works to see the fish in the light of her own humbled knowledge that to pull it out of its element is already to get it wrong, and remarkable to see how such knowledge, combined with the desire to stand before the fish in true humility, which, presumably, entails honesty—service—draws her out. She knows, I think, two things: that a fish out of water (as the saying goes) is already inaccurate, and that to leave the boat, as Marianne Moore does in her own earlier poem of the same title, is to engage in fantasy. And yet she feels compelled, because she is humbled, to get it right.

∽

Bishop goes on:

> Here and there
> his brown skin hung in strips
> like ancient wallpaper,
> and its pattern of darker brown
> was like wallpaper....

"...was like wallpaper." Simile collapses into repetition, a deadened repetition, too listless to repeat the adjective "ancient" the second time. Repetition, in Bishop's poetry, never stops intruding, because in poem after poem she finds herself pulled by two elements—humility and grandeur, the latter a vastness that only in our smallness do we comprehend. And because repetition both deepens and stalls.

It's everywhere in "At the Fishhouses": "netting" and "net" just a couple words apart; "silver"; "iridescent"; "herring"; "up"; "down and down." Each one has its own character. Each feels studied, though the study often feels like a retreat. And then, more dramatically:

> Cold dark deep and absolutely clear,
> element bearable to no mortal,
> to fish and to seals . . .

The ellipses are hers. After the correction, she trails off, retreats, then tries again. This time she pulls back even sooner, though after the ellipses something stranger persists for a few lines before she turns it, again, into a joke:

> Cold dark deep and absolutely clear,
> the clear gray icy water . . . Back, behind us,
> the dignified tall firs begin.
> Bluish, associating with their shadows,
> a million Christmas trees stand
> waiting for Christmas.

After that, the poem returns to repetition, though it's different now, more elemental—two kinds of gray, both modifying the same set of "stones," and "stones" shows up four times in five lines; and "same," which enlarges in the shift from adjective to noun—as if she's finally realized that instead of lifting off, she can go down. It's water, after all:

> The water seems suspended
> above the rounded gray and blue-gray stones.
> I have seen it over and over, the same sea, the same,

slightly, indifferently swinging above the stones,
icily free above the stones,
above the stones and then the world.

Eventually, the three terms—"cold," "dark" and "clear"—
all repeat, scattered now, along with another mention of
"stones." She goes down and down, all the way into abstraction,
all the way out to "the world." A "you" enters, rhetorical but
somehow a riskier presence than the "old man" of the long
first stanza, whom she knows how to handle, largely by limiting
herself. "You," which is to say we, is instead handled by the
sheer force of her authority, her unchecked mastery, as in the
lines above. The pretense of humility disappears.

But to say humility is a pretense isn't quite right, either. It's
a position, moral and social and, therefore, like all positions,
complicated.

≫

I'm always won over by the bus driver in "The Moose,"
his modest description of majesty: "'Curious creatures,' /
says our quiet driver, / rolling his r's. / 'Look at that, would
you.'" It's almost the end of the poem, and what follows is more
precise, but it's no more penetrating. Curious. Look at that.
Language like that is always pulling on Bishop's poems, where
the characters are far more likely to be bus drivers than tenured
professors. Where even the painter who shows up in "Poem"
and "Small Bad Painting" is somewhere between an amateur
and a craftsman. Bishop had money. She had education and
opportunity. But if she tended to leave that out of her writing,
it wasn't (or at least, wasn't primarily) to romanticize people
who had less. They mattered more to her than that, and in more
complicated, sometimes treacherous, ways.

Bishop was the kind of person who would say less, or
nothing, rather than say something untrue or out of place. (A

lot of things, for Bishop, never got said.) And she was the kind of person who feared standing out—a person for whom the double meaning of "curious" (interested but also worthy of interest: strange) meant a lot. I've never been able to give myself over to "The Sandpiper," in whose downcast eyes "The world is a mist. And then the world is / minute and vast and clear." For whom, "The tide / is higher or lower. He couldn't tell you which." It feels thinned out, in places, by a meanness meant for herself, and like several of her poems concerned with humility, its ending is both appropriate and insufficient. But it is telling, a sharpened and more severe version of Isaac Newton's self-summary, "to myself I seem to have been only like a boy playing on the sea-shore, and diverting myself in now and then finding a smoother pebble or a prettier shell than ordinary, whilst the great ocean of truth lay all undiscovered before me." "Poor bird," she mocks, in a way she would never write of the bus driver or the old man. *Poor* meaning *fool*.

᠅

And *fool* meaning me. By now, it may be apparent that this is my own self-portrait of sorts. That the Elizabeth Bishop I'm describing here is occluded and configured by my own fears about my own foolishness, and my fears, too, about how that fear has fashioned me. Humility has been, for me, a hiding place, a way to lower my center of gravity. I, too, have tended to impersonate an ordinary person, though not so much in the sense of hiding something extraordinary, like Bishop's brilliance, but of being less obviously weird, less strange, less foolish—the last of those my lifelong fear: shame.

Some of the problems of this are obvious—the life not lived, etc.—and they all apply to me. I have spent, I think, most of my life getting ready for my life, waiting for, working for, that moment when I can be safe from judgment. And the problem with that, aside from its inevitable self-harm, is that it's a lie, and that the actions it impels promote that lie, and that the lie is in part rooted in the ways that we (that I) imagine what ordinary might mean.

Consider a poem like "Manuelzinho," and how differently Bishop writes when writing of "ordinary" people in Brazil, even around the same time she was writing about the old man and the bus driver in "At the Fishhouses" and "The Moose." How far from ordinary they seem, and how little the language of those poems seems constrained by the language of those she—or, it seems important in at least one poem to say, her speaker—describes. They stand in her poems odd and exposed. She can play with them. She can judge, evaluate, stand apart—stand out—safe from being judged in return. She seems, in one regard, to see them more clearly, with less awe, than she might someone in Nova Scotia, but at the same time they have less power, less pull—less of whatever it is that might lurk behind a word like "tremendous" in her description of the "battered and venerable" fish.

And yes, she notes that the person speaking in "Manuelzinho" is "a friend of the writer," but she—Bishop—is freer here, fiercer, funnier, more at play, both as and about the friend and in relationship to the person the friend describes, than I can imagine her being in any poem set in her native New England and Nova Scotia. As she writes

> Half squatter, half tenant (no rent)—
> a sort of inheritance; white,
> in your thirties now, and supposed
> to supply me with vegetables,
> but you don't; or you won't; or you can't
> get the idea through your brain—
> the world's worst gardener since Cain.

the ordinary gravity of her work seems to relent, something that usually only happens in those poems of hers that forego narrative, or realism, or both. The poem feels unchecked, more immediate, more willing to take what it needs. Less wary of making too much (or too little) of anything. And, at least for me—and maybe for her, as well—less interesting for that.

≋

One dictionary starts off its definition of "humble" by saying what it isn't: not proud; not arrogant. There's something oppositional about humility, a resistance, an awareness of what it will not or cannot have. Even the false modesty of a phrase like "I am humbled…" seems to recognize this, to use humility as a kind of charm against boastfulness, though only so that it's then possible to boast. It's humility with the gravity turned off.

Compare the freedom of "Manuelzinho" to the opening lines of "At the Fishhouses," ruled by a decorum so strict that the poem grows edgy and odd underneath. Working to avoid calling any attention to herself, Bishop finally, after six lines, takes it to a comic extreme: "The air smells so strong of codfish / it makes one's nose run and one's eyes water." The repeated and willfully uninformative pseudo-pronoun—the awkward twice-attempted marriage of personal and universal and singular in so pedestrian an observation ("*one*'s nose run and *one*'s eyes water")—seems to have slipped in from some other, snootier, set of conventions altogether. Surely no one at the docks says "one" in that way. She's hiding so hard that she's exposed herself.

All the while, inside the careful modesty of Bishop's description, her work to honor this scene by never making it more than it is, the mannerly syntax (the information delivered one unit at a time), sense keeps slipping loose. "The five fishhouses have steeply peaked roofs / and narrow, cleated gangplanks…." Read just that far, the lines indicate that "narrow, cleated gangplanks" are merely the second of two things "the five fishhouses have." The punctuation suggests this, too: no comma after "roofs" should mean that the "and" is merely making a list. But "gangplanks" seems to change its mind, or hers: the direct object turns into a subject as we read "steeply peaked roofs / and narrow, cleated gangplanks slant up," a surprising verb, the most energetic in the poem so far. They "…slant up / to storerooms in the gables / for the wheelbarrows to be pushed up and down on." A small energy gets loose in that phrase and keeps running until the dangling preposition, so ordinary elsewhere but out of place here, brings the brief fluency to a halt.

Immediately after that, she leaps again: "All is silver." But the easy, earned grandeur tires in figure and fact: "the heavy surface of the sea, / swelling slowly as if considering spilling over, / is opaque…." What at first seems to be the beginning of a list of examples, silver things swelling into imagination, turns out to be, once again, the subject of a new sentence. The "is" lands flatly in a new line, in contrast to the aspirational "is" of "All is silver," correcting it almost, deflating: "is opaque." Short and flat and maybe not (not really) silver at all. She has to look elsewhere, repeating herself, to move on: "but the silver of the benches…."

❧

Yes . . ." that peculiar
affirmative. "Yes . . .

Among the many odd affirmations poetry can make, in addition to translating bad news into something softer than gossip, something that can keep talk meaningful and be borne more readily, is that of making familiar words more proper to experience and even the plainest terms more worthy of song.

Bishop's poetry *is* affirmative, in part because it so persuasively presents an acute mind humbling itself to articulate life on a small scale. There's often a kind of tidal patience at work in her poems, a sense of a large force moving in small increments. At times, the comfort of her poems, with their repetitions and their mostly unremarkable language deployed remarkably, feels almost parental, like the grandparents whose "peculiar / affirmative" she draws out over four gently metered stanzas: "Now, it's all right now / even to fall asleep / just as on all those nights." In such affirmations, I suspect, she's making (or repairing) a home for herself.

The paradox, though, is the humble world of her poems is made habitable by the force pressing against their smallness. The paradox is that she left the places she describes. The paradox is that these humble elements also affirm—and allow— what is large in her work, including what is occasionally vast and unfettered, almost frictionless, tremendous, grand.

≈

"...as when emotion too far exceeds its cause."

The past tense of "The Fish" seems lengthy, as if the memory has persisted out of proportion to the facts of the moment. The poem feels like an attempt to find some way of describing the fish that will both account for its persistence—for its having seemed and seeming still "tremendous"—and stay true to the actual, ordinary, scene: I caught a fish.

What does humility look or sound like in a poem? Must humble poems use humble materials: simple words, plain images, settings that don't seem to depend on wealth? Should they stay calm? Should they be unusually honest? Should the poet or speaker or both refrain from serving him or herself? And if so, if it really requires all this, can it be worth much without being at least somewhat at odds with itself?

In many of Bishop's best poems ("At the Fishhouses," "The Moose," "In the Waiting Room," maybe even in "Crusoe in England," with the implied audience that seems to motivate Crusoe's monologue) someone more apparently humble than Bishop looks on and seems almost to be listening in. In "The Fish," the fish itself—tremendous, battered, venerable, homely—exerts a similar pull.

"While his gills were breathing in / the terrible oxygen," she writes. It's her first act of sympathy, though it doesn't last, and it doesn't go far. Her imagining the air she breathes as terrible doesn't make her think that she could have just put the fish back in the water where it could breathe. Instead, after a dash cuts in, she imagines the gills in terms their ability to damage *her* flesh: "—the frightening gills, / fresh and crisp with blood, / that can cut so badly—" And when she returns to the body of the fish, she's moved from empathy to an imagination of the fish's flesh from within, cut open, all anatomy now, all fact, but she stays visible, opening the next observation with "I thought":

> I thought of the coarse white flesh
> packed in like feathers,
> the big bones and the little bones,
> the dramatic reds and blacks
> of his shiny entrails,
> and the pink swim-bladder
> like a big peony.

Two similes—the kind of thing that calls attention to itself. The two before had quickly collapsed: "like ancient wallpaper… was like wallpaper." Now you can hear her putting the brakes on herself again. Before she can even say "peony," she introduces an adjective that's willfully plain, almost childish: "a big peony." It's one of the very first adjectives we learn (*So* big!), and one of the least precise.

There are moments like that throughout "The Fish," places where Bishop begins making connections, interpreting, finding figures, then once again pushes the fish away, into the factual, the practical. You can hear it over and over again in her work, as in "Poem," where she catches herself:

> Our visions coincided—"visions" is
> too serious a word—our looks, two looks:

It's a performance of revision. She doesn't go back and write "Our looks coincided." It's important to say "visions," and to say it again, this time self-critically—to keep the "too serious" impulse in as well as the explanation of why it's wrong.

"We both knew this place," she writes a few lines earlier in "Poem," leading up to the moment of excess:

> apparently, this literal small backwater,
> looked at it long enough to memorize it,
> our years apart. How strange. And it's still loved,
> or its memory is (it must have changed a lot).

"How strange." It's like the bus driver's lines in "The Moose"—but this is Bishop talking, using one of those expressions that, like the "yes"es in "The Moose," adds nothing but acknowledgment, leaving room for all who are willing to say no more than that.

After downgrading from "visions" to "looks," Bishop seems tempted to lift off again:

> Life and the memory of it cramped,
> dim, on a piece of Bristol board,
> dim, but how live, how touching in detail
> —the little that we get for free,
> the little of our earthly trust. Not much.
> About the size of our abidance
> along with theirs: the munching cows,
> the iris, crisp and shivering, the water
> still standing from spring freshets,
> the yet-to-be-dismantled elms, the geese.

"Dim," and then "dim" again, as she starts to accelerate, revising upward: "but how live, how touching," the repetition of "how" in those unobtrusive phrases suggesting (as opposed to the slowing of just one: "How strange") that something grand is coming now, that she has finally grounded the poem carefully enough to let it soar. The language then shifts to something larger but still proper to this place, moving from plain speech into the biblical tones of "the little of our earthly trust," before pulling back again: "Not much." The unfussy "about the size," and then again the slightly archaic "abidance," with its pseudo-biblical formality. And that's the last of it. The poem retreats into humility, description, nothing more abstract than what precision can yield: animals, plants, the painting, with only "yet-to-be-dismantled" estranging and enlarging the scene before "the geese," without even a conjunction to make it feel conclusive, ends flatly, an insufficient half-rhyme reaching back toward "free."

The humility, here, seems too successful. There's too little that she'll allow herself to give. The ending feels ungenerous, if accurate in its way. I can't help feeling that it's a little romanticized, a little smaller than it would be from inside, and unable to see what true humility allows: a view of grandeur, an experience of awe. It insists on disappointment without (to my ear) seeming to acknowledge how much of that disappointment is hers.

Compare that to the ending of "2,000 Illustrations and a Complete Concordance":

> Everything only connected by "and" and "and."
> Open the book. (The gilt rubs off the edges
> of the pages and pollinates the fingertips.)
> Open the heavy book. Why couldn't we have seen
> this old Nativity while we were at it?
> —the dark ajar, the rocks breaking with light,
> an undisturbed, unbreathing flame,
> colorless, sparkless, freely fed on straw,
> and, lulled within, a family of pets,
> —and looked and looked our infant sight away.

Here again, the repetitions, the hesitancies, but this time bolder: "Open the book." She slips back into description, but she's more commanding next time: "Open the heavy book."

The visionary impulse, when it comes, comes hedged: not actually seen, only in the book. But her commitment to it, for at least three lines, is absolute, even in its contradictions and impossibilities. Even if she still needs to be honest about its impossibility, even as she gives in and mocks the image ("a family of pets"), the gift of those three lines does not recede, nor can the subsequent conclusion of the question shake off their passion, no matter how critical it is, the "looked and looked" so much more emphatic than the "'and' and 'and'" that starts the stanza on a brilliant dead note. The final erasure of "away" (itself also unreal), like the "flown" at the end of "At the Fishhouses," is not a return to the earlier restrictions, but rather an attempt to bring humility to bear on this newly dominant, still-ecstatic mode.

This is the Bishop I love most. The one who finally, partially, slips free. Though I doubt I'd love her so much were it not for the long labor from which the freedom flows.

There's always a danger in learning too much from the things we love, and so I'm wary of making too much of Bishop's humility. But I'm wary, too, of holding her too accountable for my flaws. I believe humility is a cardinal virtue, a necessary check on our arrogance and ambition, a means of acknowledging others and living more lightly on the earth. I believe, too, that it's a short walk from humility to parochialism, and that it's easy to mistake the two, so much so that we fail to recognize humility when it comes in clothing we haven't seen before—how often has white America accused others of being too flamboyant? It enables nostalgia, and it has served unjust powers with terrible frequency (though what hasn't, and what won't?)

Humility served Bishop. At times it blinded it her; often it hid much of her from view. It would have been insufficient had she been at home in it (the one likely exception, to my mind, is "The Moose"), and in those places where she gave humility the last word, her poems typically fall flat. Even "The Fish," which I've discussed at length, feels too beholden to its principles at the end. And yet: and yet, the attempt to live alertly inside the challenges of seeing something accurately ("'visions' is / too serious a word—our looks, two looks"), an act that is only possible when we submit the world to our distorting, animating, mysterious care, *is* humbling in the most profound sense: it allows us to see where we are and allows us, occasionally, to look up.

2. Philip Larkin

How many of Larkin's best poems end (or at least advance toward their endings) with him looking up—or at least out—from a room of some sort? How many of them are, in some fundamental sense, *about* rooms: small rooms, bleak rooms, single rooms? How often does he burrow into places where he feels less than at home? How much does he resist and return to the idea of "home" itself—"Home" which, he wrote, "is so sad"? That poem's ending is a lot like the final pentameter line of Bishop's "Poem," the flat, imperfect rhyme and the lack of a conjunction to lend any sense of conclusion:

> You can see how it was:
> Look at the pictures and the cutlery.
> The music in the piano stool. That vase.

But where Bishop's ending is meant to sound like a failure, this one sounds like success of a sort. Larkin seems to be relishing the bad news. There's a commanding element more akin to the conclusion of "2,000 Illustrations." And there's a heightened musicality in Larkin's measuring of the pentameter, so that the two-syllable sentence fragment lands with its own conclusive, contradictory force.

At the heart of that contradiction is, I think, the heart of much of Larkin's poetry. The sadness Larkin finds at home relies on the assumption that there *should* be happiness, a still-inscribed "joyous shot at how things ought to be, / Long fallen wide." Larkin's humility, his insistence on meagerness, verges on knowingness, and his knowingness depends on a sense of "how things ought to be" that he never really turns away from, even as he insists that nothing will actually work out that way.

≈

Continuity pulled hard on Larkin's imagination. He exclaims, in "To the Sea," "Still going on, all of it, still going on!" His warmest concluding lines offer, if not continuation, then at least the unironized wish for it: "Let it always be there." "Sent out of sight, somewhere becoming rain." Or ironized in ways that are easy to overlook: "What will survive of us is love." Even more often, his poems end in the disheartened knowledge of endings: "I just think it will happen, soon." "And age, and then only the end of age." "And dulls to distance all we are." "Never such innocence again."

Death, of course, was the great discontinuity in Larkin's imagination, the inevitable ending that at times made it almost impossible for him to go on. This has its own irony: Larkin's fear of death so diminished his experience of life at times that death's significance should have been lessened, there being so much less for it to take away.

Only in "Church Going" does death become part of a meaningful continuity. It's wrapped in a deflating irony—but continuity was always in part about diminishing things for Larkin, making the world knowable, manageable, England its own small room, so that it could then be cherished without pretense and without overwhelming him. (Death, after all, wasn't problematic just because it ended things, but also because it seemed so vast: "the total emptiness forever," he wrote in "Aubade.")

Larkin ends "Church Going" by imagining some future version of himself:

> surprising
> A hunger in himself to be more serious,

> And gravitating with it to this ground,
> Which, he once heard, was proper to grow wise in,
> If only that so many dead lie round.

The ironies are everywhere, down to the slightly comic rhyme of "surprising" and "wise in." Same goes for "he once heard," which recalls Larkin's own bemused entrance into the church at the poem's beginning, and the concluding line with its opening "if only" and the subsequent sense that this is hardly the kind of wisdom that would provide comfort. (If the "dead lie round," they are not resurrected.)

But Larkin's not kidding around. After a brilliant comic opening, he acknowledges, "Yet stop I did: in fact I often do." The final sentence unfolds with an almost courtly elegance. He introduces his future envoy in the penultimate stanza with another turn, as

> Bored, uninformed, knowing the ghostly silt
> Dispersed, yet tending to this cross of ground
> Through suburb scrub because it held unspilt
> So long and equably what since is found
> Only in separation—marriage, and birth,
> And death, and thoughts of these—for which was built
> This special shell? For, though I've no idea
> What this accoutred frowsty barn is worth,
> It pleases me to stand in silence here;

Larkin keeps turning away from his own mocking—"yet," "yet." And then there's the pivot that introduces the dependent clause in the seventh line ("For, though") suggesting that *this* time, even as he mocks the "accoutred frowsty barn," he's already planning to say something more tender. He's getting ready to say again that this compels him, to talk about its ability to hold so much of life, as he says in another phrase that diminishes without destroying, "unspilt."

But the pleasure of the poem is just as much in the diminishing, both because it makes what Larkin finds more credible and because it's such a detailed performance. Consider the first stanza:

> Once I am sure there's nothing going on
> I step inside, letting the door thud shut.
> Another church: matting, seats, and stone,
> And little books; sprawlings of flowers, cut
> For Sunday, brownish now; some brass and stuff
> Up at the holy end; the small neat organ;
> And a tense, musty, unignorable silence,
> Brewed God knows how long. Hatless, I take off
> My cycle-clips in awkward reverence.

It's an extraordinary mix of attention and apparent disinterest. That extra "and" at the start of the fourth line, a spilling over that suggests indifference—oh, and that, too. The imprecision of "brownish" and "some brass and stuff" and "God knows how long"—with "God" sounding particularly and pointedly idiomatic, given the context. The substitution of cycle clips for a hat.

Larkin's putting on a show here, and it's a hell of a show. It's also essential, like the long build up in "At the Fishouses," to the latter beauty it resists. The show, just like the humility, for Larkin, was never the point—until, to his detriment, it was.

∽

It's fair to ask, as Larkin's defenders do, why Larkin, among all the poets who have said and written and done bigoted things, has been so defined by those failures. It's also fair to ask why his defenders are so determined to insulate him from his own words. The answer is, I suspect, the same in both cases.

Larkin's own imitation of an ordinary person roots so deep in his work that, for all his originality and refusals, he becomes representative of a particular ideal—a proud parochialism that imagines itself to be universal, a version of common sense that proves its reliability by always circling back to itself. Larkin's bigotry was inextricable from that and also, at times, from the poetry itself. It gets near the heart of his achievement and speaks to the ways we blind ourselves to the reality of others— and to the way certain visions rely on that blindness.

If I'm being harsh, it's probably because Larkin, even more than Bishop, has always felt like a version of myself. He was a sentimental man who disdained sentimentality, partly because he knew he should. He was ambitious and insecure, and he worked hard to hide each impulse inside the other. He seems to have defined himself in large part through others' perceptions of him, and he preferred to spend much of his time alone as a result. He hid inside a certain posture so long his range of motion diminished. He was immediately recognizable and yet somewhat elusive. He was easily overwhelmed. He hungered for transcendence and feared it terribly. He saw most of these things about himself and hated himself for them, and he also felt superior for seeing himself so clearly—and for the ability to pick apart others that came with it.

Or so it seems to me. Larkin's bigotry frightens me because I can imagine it being mine in a way that, for example, Ezra Pound's could never be. My relationship to his poems is probably more personal than my relationship to any other poet's. For all their bleakness, they console me in a way that no other poems do. They leave me feeling simultaneously exalted and safe. They suggest, to me, that the worst of life is manageable and that beauty is near at hand. They are, for me, in their insistent pessimism, the clearest example of poetry's peculiar affirmation. I feel, at certain moments, the way you sometimes feel on vacation, alert and yet freed for a time from obligations and awareness, more at home than you would ever feel anywhere you lived.

Many years ago I was in a workshop with Brenda Hill-
man, a poet I adore and in no way resemble. "High Windows" came up and she shuddered, recalling the final lines:
"that shows / Nothing, and is nowhere, and is endless." Until
that moment, I'd never considered the possibility that the
poem's ending might be bleak. To be honest, I still can't hear
it that way. I can't even get close.

Maybe it's the "sun-comprehending glass" that contains that
endlessness, my imagination of the room in which such "deep
blue air" might enter through those windows, enlarging the
confined space in which such endlessness might come, suddenly,
to mind. It feels like a relief to me, a sudden and profound (and
also safe) evasion of the social world in which everyone (or,
at least, "everyone young") is "going down the long slide //
To happiness, endlessly." (How much bleaker *that* endlessness
seems to me, its going forever down into the world of others
and expectations and happiness that will never materialize.)
A relief from the awareness of yourself as having also been
watched at one point, and misunderstood just as badly. (Like I
said, I see a lot of myself in Larkin.)

Andrew Motion has written of the "number of moments"
in Larkin's work, the ending of "High Windows" among them,
that "manage to transcend the flow of contingent time altogether." It's not just "contingent time," though—it's social
contingency, too. Humility, for Larkin, was an important part
of managing (and, when possible, evading) that contingency.
I always imagine the high windows *he* imagines being a part
of one of the small bedrooms he rented over most of his
adult life, the kind he described in "Mr. Bleaney." (Though
in that poem, the windows initially look down, only exposing
clouds once Larkin has entered, inside the allowances of "if,"
Bleaney's imagined perspective from the unimaginable past.)

In "Mr. Bleaney," too, Larkin works in descriptions that are
at once off-hand and precisely observed. (The first starts off as
if it will be an unpredicated list. The second is. Both end without
the expected conjunction.) "Flowered curtains, thin and frayed,

/ Fall to within five inches of the sill, // Whose window shows a strip of building land, / Tussocky, littered." "Bed, upright chair, sixty-watt bulb, no hook / Behind the door, no room for books or bags—" He follows the latter with his response, "'I'll take it," a kind of self-mockery that implicates him in the notion that "how we live measures our own nature."

"Mr. Bleaney" ends in its own irresolution: "I don't know." But as with the conclusion of "The Old Fools" ("Well, / We shall find out") the suggestion is that he does know. You couldn't help but see, Larkin thinks, how a room like that judges you. It's worth noting that the actual character Mr. Bleaney, unlike the nondescript woman who shows him the room, never appears in the poem. For all that his poems are set in the ordinary world of work and town, Larkin's most noteworthy characters are all off-stage, where they won't interfere with things. Actual, specific people would need too much, entail a second audience, and for better and worse, Larkin's poetry depends on a careful management of his audience. It requires an audience that is, at least in its responses, predictable: uniform.

(Here, too, I'm superimposing myself. I hate to mix different groups of friends because it's so hard to keep my balance, trying to be the person each one of them might want me to be. But I don't think I'm *just* superimposing it. As in his life outside of writing, Larkin put a lot of work into his poses, and the poses mitigate against the same perceptions, so much so that it's easy to imagine Kingsley Amis, Larkin's cooler and in many ways colder friend, lurking on the other end of his poems. And so much so that it's easy for me to imagine where my own hunger for a uniform, predictable audience might have carried me and god, who knows, maybe someday will.)

Like Bishop, Larkin spent much of his childhood feeling far from at home in the world, and he seems to have constructed a sense of self—as so many of us who grow up out of place do—based on others' responses to him. And like Bishop, he seems to have spent much of his life trying to build places in which his cares and impulses could fit in, as well as standing out.

Part of what makes Larkin so fascinating—so extraordinary—is that his impersonation of ordinary was so much more agile than ordinary itself. In the rooms of his poems—both the rooms they describe and their elegantly rhymed stanzas—Larkin moves, once you've tared the enabling, essential, sourness and cynicism, with more grace than seem imaginable in so hunched a posture as he presents. He's like the star actor on whose face the life of the character is richer than it would ever be on the face of the character her or himself. And so for those of us who find some version of our humbled, if not actually humble, selves in his poems, the encounter can be strangely (and, in some cases, frighteningly) ennobling.

❧

"Aubade" was the last good poem Larkin would write. It was also the last great poem he would write, a final, vibrant, creation in the expansive mode that produced so much of his best work. It opens with Larkin working in a continuous present tense, the same room where he wakes to his failures to be more alive, as death approaches, night after night. As in his actual life, Larkin is trapped inside his performance: "I work all day, and get half-drunk at night."

How Larkinesque an opening it is, calling back from decades earlier the opening of his first poem in this style, "Church Going." Even the "half" of "half-drunk" feels right, a self-effacement diminished lest it turn into a boast. It's reminiscent of the title of Larkin's first important book: *The Less Deceived.*

Seamus Heaney complained that "Aubade" "does not hold the lyre up in the face of the gods of the underworld; it does not make the Orphic effort to haul life back up the slope against all odds." The statement seems like an uncharacteristic failure of imagination on Heaney's part. (Whether the standard is even valid is an argument for another book.) For Heaney, the idea that such a poem could serve the living was incomprehensible.

Warmer consolations served Heaney, who was far more available to joy and more capable of imagining redemption. (His *North* was a remarkable example of just the type of heroic, Orphic effort he thought Larkin had neglected.) But "Aubade" is a consolation for the disconsolate, a poem that lifts into markedly social language the elements of despair that had calcified around Larkin's imagination by that time. It was Larkin's last beautiful act of dancing through the by-then shrinking room he had spent much of a lifetime erecting around himself. It was a denial of reality as he saw it grounded in something uncompromisingly real, and in that sense not so different from the concluding lines of "Church Going." It brought what Larkin saw as the utter isolation (even from oneself: "Not to be here, / Not to be anywhere, / And soon") of death into the continuity of speech. In making his fear extraordinary, he also makes it conventional:

> I work all day, and get half-drunk at night.
> Waking at four to soundless dark, I stare.
> In time the curtain-edges will grow light.
> Till then I see what's really always there:
> Unresting death, a whole day nearer now,
> Making all thought impossible but how
> And where and when I shall myself die.
> Arid interrogation: yet the dread
> Of dying, and being dead,
> Flashes afresh to hold and horrify.

"Making all thought impossible but how / And where and when I shall myself die." But the poem stands outside that thought, those nights. The poem makes room for other thoughts.

How quickly "Aubade" throws off the humility of "I work all day and get half-drunk at night." How fast and how thoroughly the room dissolves into a confident universaliz-ing. After that first stanza, the first-person singular disappears, and Larkin instead speaks for a "we" that clearly means everyone—or everyone, he might say, who's honest enough to admit to the truth.

You can see why the poem would have angered Heaney. Larkin's not just trying to articulate his fear; he's arguing for its accuracy as an image of the world. The poem gets condescending: "Religion used to try, / That vast, moth-eaten musical brocade / Created to pretend we never die...." As those lines continue, there's an astonishing fluency that feels almost like a delight in the horrible news that proves his point:

> And specious stuff that says *No rational being*
> *Can fear a thing it will not feel,* not seeing
> That this is what we fear—no sight, no sound,
> No touch or taste or smell, nothing to think with,
> Nothing to love or link with,
> The anesthetic from which none come round.

The room is gone. The narrative circumstance is gone. The *fear* is gone. This is straight argument, and it relieves Larkin's burden for a bit. (He even laments the loss of a social and love life he almost never celebrated in poetry.) He's alive here, arguing for death.

That's not to say that "Aubade" is a dishonest poem. I actually think it's one of Larkin's most honest poems—not because of what it says, though it matters to me that he makes that so sayable—but because he says it so early in the poem. The modesty that Larkin usually spends much of the poem erecting (which is often one of the pleasures of his poetry) falls away after the third line. When the trappings of humility return in the final stanza, as he nods, briefly, to the narrative circumstance, they mean something else altogether. This is now the "uncaring / Intricate rented world," and its plain materials, paradoxically, gleam with meaning:

> Slowly light strengthens, and the room takes shape.
> It stands plain as a wardrobe, what we know,
> Have always known, know that we can't escape,
> Yet can't accept.

I do not doubt that this appalls most. It thrills me, though. Not because I want to convince anyone to look at the world this way, but because one of the reasons I go to poetry is a desire to hear the unspeakable spoken well. To make it seem a little more human—and a little more than human, too: to bring it into a version of our voices that is more agile and extraordinary than much of what we ordinarily share.

It's anger, I think, that fuels the poem, far more than fear—frustration with all the consolations that felt like refusals to acknowledge his fear. And it was a kind of anger that, I think, he could only follow so freely in a poem that late in his life. Just as he could no longer write the kind of poems he used to write, having lived so long inside his defenses that they had become a kind of permanent armor, stiffening his movements but indistinguishable, especially to him, from himself—just as he could no longer write those poems this far into his life, I doubt he could have written a poem like this back then, when the door to the universal was, for him, at most a window, small and out of reach. The continuities between the two are obvious, but Larkin has stopped imagining those who might dislike him except as people to be dismissed.

You could make too much of this. I adore this poem and have no real problems with it. Sure, the dig at religion seems petty, but it's also fun—sharp, witty. (And harmless, I think; religion seems to have survived Larkin's disdain.) But I think it also reveals some of the same forces that enabled Larkin, elsewhere, at his bigoted worst. And in that, it also reveals one of the risks of humility as an enabling pose.

I love the first-person plural in poems—its ambition and risk and tension. I love it for what it reaches toward and what its faltering can remind us of. But it can also be facile, and facility is, I think, something many of us hunger for. I do, and I think Larkin did as well. One of the pleasures of Larkin's poems, and Bishop's, too, is the agile and intricate work they undertake in trying to make their way to that moment when the coefficient of friction is finally overcome and the poem accelerates into something simultaneously hard-earned and apparently easy. More often than not, the awareness of others who disagree with us or stand outside of the "we" that we reflexively employ interrupts or simply prohibits such ease. It prohibits fluency. It makes the "we" waver until our sense of who "we" are grows.

As Larkin aged and the world around him became more aware of its own complexity, his sense of audience risked becoming unmanageable. The "we" he had worked so hard to construct, poem to poem, room by room—and the particular version of humility that had allowed him to stand erect—became, as did England's dominant image of itself, more aware, more alert to all of England that "England" did not include. And Larkin, who had put so much of himself into that ideal, reacted as so many do in that situation: he doubled down on his blindness. Larkin, who longed for continuity, and who so often invested his ideal of continuity in an image of humble English life, looked at anyone who threatened its continuity as a threat. In "Going, Going," he was able to return it to a kind of pastoral. The final image could resonate with one strand of our present environmentalism:

> Most things are never meant.
> This won't be, most likely: but greeds
> And garbage are too thick-strewn
> To be swept up now, or invent
> Excuses that make them all needs.
> I just think it will happen, soon.

So, too, could the lovely and unusually loving "Show Saturday," which concludes:

Let it stay hidden there like strength, below
Sale-bills and swindling; something people do,
Not noticing how time's rolling smithy-smoke
Shadows much greater gestures; something they share
That breaks ancestrally each year into
Regenerate union. Let it always be there.

In such poems, Larkin finds a place for that hunger, and
the humility becomes (to use Larkin' astonishing adjective) "regenerate." There's no need to dismiss these poems because of
the uses to which they could be put—no need to do away with
humility, or even the performance of humility (which can at
least allow us a momentary scent of the earth), simply because
it can be exploited. All things can. But neither does it makes
sense to keep from them the news of the company they kept in
Larkin's imagination and, sometimes, in the poems themselves.

"Show Saturday" ends in repetition, "Let it stay hidden
there like strength" (how odd, and perhaps how telling, that
he presents "strength" as something hidden) becoming "Let it
always be there," the latter plainer and more emphatic, giving
the impression that he has finally, in the midst of that last enu-
meration, managed to hone it all down to the essential. A little
like Bishop at the end of "At the Fishhouses," he's arrived at a
universal by going down—where the universe also is.

We are now at a moment in American life when the worst
of us is convulsing loudly, angrily, menacingly. This is obviously not the place to examine the ascendancy of Donald Trump
or even the proliferation of Confederate flags I see twice a
day, driving to and from the school where I teach. Past failures prolonged and resurrected, injustice woven so thoroughly
into all of American life that parts of American life must be
completely unstitched to do away with them. There is, as many
have already written, no true version of American history that
is not also the history of plunder. This is not that essay. But
it's worth saying, I think, that the awareness of a similar un-

stitching stands just outside of a poem like "Show Saturday."
The people there do not notice, Larkin says, what he does:
"time's rolling smithy-smoke." But they will notice the change,
in years to come, that Larkin had by then already noticed at the
university where he worked. Some of them will respond with
grace and kindness, with versions of humility that say I am no
more entitled to this country than anyone else. Others will not,
and some of those will invoke humility in trying to protect
themselves from a complicating awareness of others as just as
English as them.

   If poetry is in part a place where the otherwise-intolerable
might, with enough care, eventually be said—if it is, at times,
an attempt to answer the at-first-inexplicable pull of an emotion that seems to exceed its cause—then humility is essential
if it will ever be possible to get both that impulse and the larger reality in which it's felt—fish and feeling—right. And if the
desire to say, of the things I love, "Let it always be there," is
to be honored, then I must be humble enough to acknowledge
that even humility might blind me to what "it" entails. And I
must admit, too, how often performances of humility begin in
something actually humble, in ordinary human fear.

   The ecstatic moments in both Bishop and Larkin—the
ones their humility so often seems to be preparing for—
achieve their own humility as well: "self-forgetful," as Bishop
once described the pleasure of writing in a letter to a friend.
The paradox of it almost shines, perilous and redemptive at
once: We are delighted by unawareness of the very being that
enjoys the unawareness of itself. "And that much," as Larkin
wrote in "Church Going," with a small, playful sneer at the
world he couldn't bear to lose, "never can be obsolete."

"Where There is Estrangment, There is Little Peace": On Kindness

Kindness is, at its furthest reaches, a thorough engagement of the self in an act of self-abnegation. It's one's own absence made flesh in the acceptance of another's reality. It is an exercise of the imagination. Etymologically, it refers to making others kin, recognizing them as versions of ourselves, of the selves we set aside. It is also, therefore, a reimagination of ourselves. In *On Kindness*, Adam Phillips and Barbara Taylor define it as "the ability to bear the vulnerability of others, and therefore of oneself," and even as they argue for its place among the fundamental pleasures and essential enablers of our social lives, they continue to suggest both its complication and its cost. "Bearing other people's vulnerability," they continue, "which means sharing in it imaginatively and practically without needing to get rid of it, to yank people out of it—entails being able to bear one's own."

To act with kindness, we must imagine that someone else is as worthy of our care as we are ourselves—and often, in the very moment of that action, to value them more than ourselves. It is eccentric, in a literal sense. It asks us to move through a world in which we do not, however briefly, stand at the center of our own concern. And that replacement of our regard, as Phillips and Taylor note, can alter and open us in lasting and sometimes-dangerous ways:

> Real kindness is an exchange with essentially unpredictable consequences. It is a risk precisely because it mingles our needs and desires with the needs and desires of others, in a way that so-called self-interest never can. (The notion of self-interest implies that we always know what we want, by knowing what the self is and what its interests are. It forecloses discovery.) Kindness is a way of knowing people beyond our understanding of them. By

involving us with strangers (even with "foreigners" thousands of miles away), as well as with intimates, it is potentially far more promiscuous than sexuality.

Promiscuous, maybe, but not easy, not always. There is a form of kindness that seems natural, especially when you're already surrounded by it. In the right situation, it can become habitual, spontaneous, simple, self-generating. That's not the type of kindness I'm interested in here. Such easy belonging, like happiness, doesn't show up on the page. Too similar to its surrounding to stand out by itself, it might show itself in its effects—a greater faith in people, a more immediate availability to the abundance of experience, a greater ease in imagining that such abundance is or could be available to all, a kind of health, a certain vitality, even. But as a literary virtue, it's most likely to remain inert or to veer into self-congratulation. Some other virtue must seep into it before it picks up any color of its own.

But there are poems that seem—that *feel*—kind. Whose movement makes me feel somehow safer, more cared for, more visible. There are poems in which it seems possible to shelter, that present a self in the act of (rather than the announcement of) making itself available to someone else. It seems peculiar. If kindness, as Phillips and Taylor argue, extends toward the particularity of another, the poem cannot be kind to me. The necessary generality of its audience precludes kindness on those terms. It is only in its investment in the particularity of some individual, whose particularity makes them audibly not me, that the poem can show me kindness.

But recording one's acts of kindness toward someone else doesn't read as kindness, as that makes the poem into a boast, its actual act, speaking, a form of self-regard. And even de-scribing the kindness of another doesn't do it, not by itself. A poem can only embody—and thereby offer—kindness if its own and only actions, speaking, singing, thinking, become credible activities of giving oneself over to another, if that giving over is embodied in the poem, in the senses, the physical movements it makes on the page, in the mouth, in the ears, in our imagined vision of a scene. It can only happen if the self remains present enough that we can feel it resisting its own presence and pull. We have to, I think, *feel* the work of kindness in the poem, the poet (or, if the speaker seems sufficiently real, then the speaker will do) pulling him or herself away from his or her own regard, becoming eccentric, muted—audibly. Without being asked to carry it (though we may nonetheless want to take it up), we have to feel the weight of what's given up.

No book of poems has struck me as kind quite as much as Spencer Reece's second, *The Road to Emmaus*. Reece became a priest between the publication of his first and second books, and *The Road to Emmaus* is a Christian book, as well as being deeply engaged with Reece's queerness—and the queerness of others, too. The book feels disciplined, in the religious sense of the term—engaged in a practice that attempts to bend one's will toward holiness over time—but the sanctity it bends toward is itself queer. Reece treats his Christ as an emblem of marginalization whose passion for others roots in his mortification at others' hands. In one poem Reece makes the metaphor explicit, describing the cross he wears after graduating from the seminary, its Jesus "a man I now relied on— / paradoxically bound and free— / a childless, bachelor Jew, slightly feminine."

That combination twines throughout the book, and Reece's own suffering stays audible in the undercurrent of its concerns, his discipline pushing him toward compassion for others and compassion for himself. The title poem, a long, slow narrative in seven parts, features three characters in addition to Reece, each from a different period of Reece's life, but all of them present because of his inability to resolve his relationship to one of them, Durell, an aging, self-loathing gay man from a rich family who had descended into poverty and served as Reece's sponsor in AA when Reece was still fairly young.

Sister Ann, the Franciscan counselor Reece visited for several years "in her small office, at the Cenacle Retreat House, / right off Dixie Highway in Lantana, Florida," is the poem's primary model of kindness. She gets the least description of anyone in "The Road to Emmaus." Two lines at the start of the third stanza ("Sister Ann's face was open, fragile— / parts were chipped like on a recovered fresco.") make up the first of only two descriptions of her; her kindness is imagined partly in her ability to disappear from view (a view that may have overlooked her throughout much of her life, given both the role of women in the church and our habit, as a society, of leaving the work of kindness to women). But she speaks often, occasionally quoted, more often paraphrased, her language so much the language of the poem itself that her statements blend into Reece's words. Occasionally, she offers a principle that punctuates a stanza, pausing the poem's forward motion to speak for the poem as a whole: "Listening, Sister Ann said, is a memorable form of love."

In that moment, she is responding to Reece's comments on Durell. The lines before it read:

> Another way of saying it was that when he was with me,
> on the phone, then and only then did he seem to move
>   in truth,
> and in his truths, reprimanding and hard,
> he was made more singular. Maybe that was it.
> Whatever the case, he listened, he listened to me.
> I missed his listening.

And before that, Reece writes:

> He matched my telling with listening, advising,
> and more listening, mostly over the phone,
> and the more he listened the more he was alone.
> "Why was that?" Sister Ann asked.
> It was some sort of offering, perhaps.

At times it seemed he needed to guarantee a pardon,
that old Catholic idea of indulgences
lurked somewhere there unspoken,
as if he believed a larger offering might guarantee a
    larger pardon.
Such a task demanded his increased singleness.
Yes, that was true. Or was it?
I had trouble settling on the right words with Sister Ann.
Many of my words were not exactly right, the syntax
    awkward.
I kept having trouble translating Durell, so much I
    guessed.

Durell's kindness, it sometimes seems, has left Reece with an unpayable debt. That's partly because it was so total that it rendered him partly invisible—while Reece, so young, was blind to it at the time. It's also, in part, because the kindness was Durell's complicated and imperfect way of compensating for his own flaws, both real and perceived. "The Road to Emmaus" tries, from the present, to listen to the past, to hear and see Durell, an act it can only undertake by adding more speech from Reece. The poem is so muted, so paradoxical, its hunger so audible, its carefulness an image at once of his care for Durell and of his own restlessness under the burden of his belatedness in seeing what he didn't hear at the time.

Durell, of course, can't receive the gift. (And not only because he died long ago: "poetry offered him no solutions," Reece says.) The poem can't hear him, either, and not just because it's too late. Poems speak. Even a poem composed entirely of someone else's words isn't exactly listening; it's making something of those words, one's own. But that doesn't make the *attempt* to listen insincere or unimportant. Its commitment to hearing, retrospectively, what Durell didn't say, alongside the unruffled acknowledgment of its insufficiency—"the syntax awkward" Reece writes inside of sentences that remain composed, their faint, gentle meter scoring the patience of the attempt—is so specific to Durell that it does become available to us (or, at least, to me). And it becomes available, I think, to Reece as well.

The first section ends with a line that sounds like Sister Ann but apparently isn't: "Where there is estrangement there is little peace." It comes at the end of Reece's recounting of the biblical story he takes for the poem's title. After his two lines describing Sister Ann he had looked above her head to "a garish postcard of the Emmaus scene" and then slipped into the that story. Unaware that the stranger walking with them is Jesus, resurrected, two men argue about his disappearance from the tomb. Reece cuts it off with them still arguing, before Jesus has revealed himself. The more I look at that line—and I seem to look at it a lot—the more important "estrangement," with its encapsulation of strangeness, feels.

It's one of the challenges of kindness, in which we offer up ourselves as sanctuary to someone else who is unable, in him or herself, to feel at home: We are, in our own offerings, imperfect. We invite someone into the flawed shelter of our own beings, sometimes in hope that such habitation will improve us. Our offer might be rejected, the vessel unappealing, the offer awkward or needy. The shelter itself might be damaged by a too-careless habitation. But it is also possible that we will diminish our own estrangement—our strangeness—or the estrangement of those who accept and move in.

I wonder how much of the mystery that keeps pulling Reece back to Durell resides in his imperfect awareness (then) of Durell's profound estrangement. His sheltering in Durell's care was partly a move from his own estrangement into the estrangement of someone else. And the mystery, too, that in doing so, he was healed a little. That Durell, self-fashioned from broken parts, wearing support hose, worried about blood clots, unable to admit to his own sexuality, hating blacks and Jews "even though the men he loved were blacks and Jews," impoverished, "unemployable," absurd, could give health, having none himself. "He had taught me… what? To live? Not to wince in the mirror?" With characteristic quiet, a simple phrase gently interrupting the sentence's forward motion then yielding to it, Reece renders the complication of Durell's gift in Sister Ann's words:

> A decorum of opprobrium kept him whole,
> and so he guarded himself with intensity.
> Maybe, Sister Ann suggested, he was guarding me.

At the end of the section in which Sister Ann is described at greater length—about five lines set in their last meeting as the remaining nuns prepared to move away—Reece concludes, uncharacteristically, with the words of someone other than Sister Ann or Durell. It comes at the end of Sister Ann's attempt to answer his question ("'What caused him to remain? / Why did he want freedom for me?'") with another biblical story:

> Sister Ann spoke then of the Gospel of John
> and the Samaritan woman at the well,
> the one married nearly as many times as Elizabeth Taylor,
> and how when Christ listened to her she became the
>   first evangelist.
> It was Christ's longest conversation with anyone Sister
>   Ann said.
> The Samaritan woman's life changed because Christ
>   listened to her.
>
> John K., from the meetings, dead now too, once said:
> "Oh, I knew Durell. He was odd. But we're all odd you
>   know."
> All I know now
> is the more he loved me the more I loved the world.

For what, in Sister Ann's explanation, might Reece evangelize? For Christianity, maybe, but the metaphor puts Durell in the role of Christ, and the juxtaposition of John K.'s emphasis on oddity—an imperfect synonym for queerness, certainly, but a synonym nonetheless—as well as Reece's mention of Elizabeth Taylor (the poem's second section ends, "Imperious, behind prism-like trifocals, / quietly he said to me, 'I've grown as fat as Elizabeth Taylor.'") makes the Christian paradox more likely metaphorical: as Jesus died so that people might live, Durell, it seems, gave a belonging he did not have. Nearly homeless himself, he made Reece at home in the world. The poem's impossible challenge (but wouldn't Durell's task have seemed impossible, too?) is to return that gift, making Durell more present and less strange, giving *him*, belatedly, a home. Sister Ann suggests that the task is instead to give both Durell's story and his gift to others equally in need of it, something Reece may do at less cost to himself, having already been partly healed. It is also, I suspect, what Sister Ann hoped him to do with the gift of her listening, for which she refused pay ("but donations, / yes, donations were appreciated"). And so again the paradox flares up—Reece can only answer the ethical impulse to heal Durrell by attempting the impossible so doggedly that it ends up achieving a different ethical end, healing us.

The poem concludes with a story he wished to tell Sister Ann but couldn't, having by then lost track of her. Durell's sister finds Reece and invites him to visit her, supposedly so that she can give him some of Durell's things. They sit and talk "by the pool in her gated country club." The sister failed Durell, and she seems to want some absolution, or at least some understanding, from Reece. But she cannot, even after his death, bring Durell into her world:

> I told her he often said his life had been a failure,
> I tried to convince him otherwise, but he never believed me.
> Half a century ago, she broke off contact.
> Her protracted estrangement made her look ill.
> "Please, please," she said.
> Her voice trailed off,
> although what she was pleading for was not clear.
> No, no, she did not want her grandchildren to know.

It is profoundly sad, but not as angering as it should be. She doesn't ask for forgiveness, and Reece doesn't offer it, but he does listen for as long as she talks, and she seems compelled by his listening. He seems to do his best to see her honestly, neither judging her nor denying what she has done or is doing. And she, too, he says, has been estranged, an assertion that implies that Durell, even in his exile from his family and, quite often, from himself, remains central, too—that there is no single center, in a world of estrangement, toward which one can move.

Time seems to spread out over the scene, a kind of spaciousness. Immediately before, he writes, echoing the causal ratios of earlier lines ("and the more he listened the more he was alone"; "His compliments had increased the more his life failed"; "the more he loved me the more I loved the world"):

> "People can be cruel," she said.
> She felt he had never adjusted to cruelty
> as if cruelty was something that one needed to adjust to.
> Later, he was picked up for charges of soliciting sex.
> And the more she told me, the less I knew.
> All about us, a stillness began to displace the light
> and Durell was there, and no longer there, staining that
>   stillness.
> After an estrangement ends there comes a great stillness,
> the greater the estrangement the greater the stillness.
> Across the parking lot, a gate rattled.

Reece doesn't say what estrangement has ended. His from Durell? The sister's from Durell? His from the sister? Instead, he once again shifts his attention, returning these broad claims to the momentary world of inconsequence they enlarge. Following it, the final stanza feels bittersweet. The stillness that comes at the end of estrangement leaves them separate ("as if the world would always be / an endless pair of separated things," Reece writes). Part of the poem's remarkable patience, its graceful arrangement of time and information, one thing at a time, is an enactment of kindness, its insistent particularity, its requirement that we make ourselves available to the needs and complexities of one person, to make that person central, to score ourselves to them in time—which means in part making room for the ways in which their lives enlarge, the ways they—we—want to be part of something larger, truer, less purely peculiar, less estranged. (In doing so we are likely to be changed, which sometimes we want and sometimes we fear—and sometimes both). The audible patience records Reece's effort to get Durell right as he tries out perspectives that would make both his residency in Durell's kindness and Durell himself finally right. It records him seeking an image accurate enough to shelter, to ratify, both Durell and the kindness that he granted Reece.

The problem with this, beyond the fact that Durell is no longer there to receive the comfort, is that it's hard to say who Durell was without condescending to him. If the poem intends to see him clearly enough to counter his terrible loneliness, then who, exactly, should it see? The person he might have been had he not been so mercilessly broken? The person he became and was often ashamed of? The person he was in his kindness, which did nothing to assuage his loneliness? Durell would have hated pity. He would have hated anyone peering through the threadbare grandeur he wore. And yet to accept that is to miss him, too, to become complicit in a lie not even he believed—and that increased his estrangement as he aged.

People can be, as Durell's sister says, cruel. We fear isolation, humiliation, loneliness. Late in the book's last poem, Reece writes, "There was no more time to hate ourselves." Durell hated himself. Others hated Durell. The poem doesn't quite ennoble him; it couldn't do that without leaving him behind. But it seems, paradoxically, to listen to him with love. Among the images of Durell that it offers is Reece's ability to listen to him without growing lonely in the way that Durell, in listening, always did. Being kind can help to heal us. It didn't heal Durell. But being kind enlarged him, allowing him to give that which he did not have. And it allowed Reece, decades later, to look back on him with love that somehow eases my estrangement—which is different from Durell's, and less—because it creates an image of the world that is more persuasive, more beautiful, more encompassing, more alert—more real—and in which the fundamental value is not any of the things that we hope will bring us love but rather love itself.

~

The sister, while also a specific person, stands in for the world that wounded Durell. Reece meets her years after the wounding—which became so much a part of Durell that even his attempts to protect himself deepened them—finally ended in the only way that it could: with Durell's death, many years ago. I find it hard to say whether Reece is kind to her. He's not *unkind*, and he does listen to her, but I'm not sure he wants to be kind to her in the manner that he wants to be toward Durell. Maybe it's best to say that he's as kind as he can be while still holding Durell in mind. Anything more would mean displacing him.

But what about situations where the harm is ongoing? These are the moments when kindness is hardest to calculate. Does kindness, in a world where people *are* cruel, require us to refuse kindness to those who are cruel? Is unkindness a means of creating a kinder world? Of being kinder to those who need our kindness most?

Gwendolyn Brooks' "The Sundays of Satin Legs Smith" sounds profoundly different from "The Road to Emmaus." It is, by design, noisy, playful, frequently delighting in its own mastery—showy. The opening sentence is almost comically rich: "Inamoratas, with an approbation, / Bestowed his title." Notably, Smith seems to be unreal, a stand-in for actual people he resembles. Other than Brooks and the briefly mentioned, long-dead European artists (Grieg, Brahms, etc.), the only potentially real person in the poem is the reader, whom Brooks addresses at length and often. Kindness must be enacted in the real world, with real people. And so to talk about kindness in "Satin Legs Smith" is to talk in part about the real people it entails: me, or you, and Brooks.

It's not just that the poem doesn't listen to me, it's that it confers an identity on me, one that makes me grotesque. I am the person who has prepared to judge Smith for his excesses—for his life of sex, his gaudy clothes, his large expenditures on cheap forms of artifice, *his* cheapness, his tawdriness. The judgments practically write themselves. They are the script for, years after Brooks wrote the poem, political diatribes about "welfare queens," the supposed cultural depravity of "the inner city," rants, dressed up in decorum and morality, about hip-hop.

For eleven lines, the poem simply describes Smith. (Though the descriptions themselves are not at all simple: with a few exceptions, the poem refuses simplicity as a betrayal of Smith, for whom it is essential "[t]hat no performance may be plain or vain.") And then, having peered for a moment behind Smith's display ("He sheds, with his pajamas, shabby days. / And his desertedness, his intricate fear, the / Postponed resentments and the prim precautions."), having seen him naked, nearly—having seen the underlying shabbiness, a state far more vulnerable for him than nakedness— she seems to notice the reader, imagine the reader, the reader's readiness to judge him for being garish, for the perceived cheapness of all he wears.

"Now, at his bath," she asks, addressing for the first time the audience that has assumed an air of superiority to Smith, "would you deny him lavender / Or take away the power of his pine?" Soon, Brooks will write of "us" ("Let us proceed. Let us inspect, together....") with palpable condescension, the arm around your shoulder that means to remind you that you're not the one in charge. But that can only come after she's set "you" straight—after she has made clear just where "your" argument for him to be more refined must lead. The lines leave an unsettling awareness in their wake, of the real work admiration for Satin Legs Smith doesn't do. "You might as well," she says twice. You might as well leave him this:

> You might as well—
> Unless you care to set the world a-boil
> And do a lot of equalizing things,
> Remove a little ermine, say, from kings,
> Shake hands with paupers and appoint them men,
> For instance—certainly you might as well
> Leave him his lotion, lavender and oil.

The reality here is that I cannot deny him anything (though I *could* work to "do a lot of equalizing things"). But the question is a real engagement of what I *can* do without putting the poem aside. I have the chance to decide whether or not I will be that "you." And Brooks gives me plenty of reason not to be him— not only the seamless integration of rhetorical precision and poetic abundance, but also the delight of watching her mock the "you" I choose not to be:

> What smelly substitute, heady as wine,
> Would you provide? life must be aromatic.
> There must be scent, somehow there must be some.
> Would you have flowers in his life? suggest
> Asters? a Really Good geranium?
> A white carnation? would you prescribe a Show
> With the cold lilies, formal chrysanthemum
> Magnificence, poinsettias, and emphatic
> Red of prize roses? might his happiest
> Alternative (you muse) be, after all,
> A bit of gentle garden in the best
> Of taste and straight tradition?

As she grows more assertive toward "you," she also seems to separate from Smith in a way that lets her offer him something plainer, gentler—more kind. "There must be scent," she writes almost plaintively, "somehow there must be some." And then again, right away:

> Maybe so.
> But you forget, or did you ever know,
> His heritage of cabbage and pigtails,
> Old intimacy with alleys, garbage pails,
> Down in the deep (but always beautiful) South
> Where roses blush their blithest (it is said)
> And sweet magnolias put Chanel to shame.

Notes of sarcasm slice through these lines, but those two lines of listing that begin with "His heritage…" seem to place her in a state of unadornment where Smith would never choose to stand. She seems to stand in for him at that moment. And so maybe the mocking of "you," which is delicious once I have decided not to be him, or her, is essential—maybe the work of refusing that person is necessary to caring for Smith, and if I take pleasure in it, maybe that's just about me. It's not, I don't think, about Smith, whose need to present himself as worthy has nothing to do with poems, or fans of Tschaikovsky. That's about the people who might be reading Brooks just after World War II, the people whose praise for her would often have its own air of condescension. And maybe it's also a kind of compensation, too—in a world where there must be scent.

She had already finished *A Street in Bronzeville* when she wrote "The Sundays of Satin Legs Smith," responding to Richard Wright's observation that important books of poems typically featured a long poem that unified the book. And so the poem begins as Brooks' own claim to consequence, made in terms of someone so thoroughly unlike her, and yet so vulnerable to the same dismissals she would come to think she had too readily acceded to, writing too deeply inside a tradition she would go on, to a limited extent, to reject.

As with Reece's rendering of Durell, Brooks' attempt to ennoble Smith is complicated by the divide between the self-image he aspired to and the terms in which he might be understood. The poem's language, which relishes bright displays, is nonetheless not Smith's. The poem is not for him, and so it leaves him behind even as it presents him, just as "The Road to Emmaus" does Durell. At times, in explaining the deprivation and humiliations Smith's showiness both transforms and denies, Brooks implies that the showiness requires excuse, accepting, implicitly, "your" impression of him as gaudy or cheap. Brooks also seems to recognize him as an artist, treating his transformation of circumstance as a work of extraordinary skill. Her admiration for that never seems feigned; her presentation of it feels too complete, including the poem's beautiful, slightly settled, almost unequivocal ending in Smith's delight, and ending in a language that no longer seems committed to creating an abundance of its own.

The last three stanzas soften and trail off. Smith disappears from view, and instead we see what he receives—see, maybe, through his eyes. The final lines about the woman's body are both beautiful and, if I step away from Smith, potentially worrying. The poem has so given itself over to his satisfaction that she, whoever she is, becomes nothing more than that.

At Joe's Eats

You get your fish or chicken on meat platters.
With coleslaw, macaroni, candied sweets,
Coffee and apple pie. You go out full.
(The end is—isn't it?—all that really matters.)

And even and intrepid come
The tender boots of night to home.

Her body is like new brown bread
Under the Woolworth mignonette.
Her body is a honey bowl
Whose waiting honey is deep and hot,
Her body is like summer earth,
Receptive, soft, and absolute ...

That last stanza is, in a sense, the logical extreme of the poem's argument in favor of Smith's pleasure, his art, and yet it also seems like an invitation to wariness: there are others here to be recognized, too. The woman is cherished in a moment that she seems to have wanted as much as he. She is seen in terms flattering to her, but terms that are also, as they trail off into sex and its welcome erasures, incomplete.

And yet those last three stanzas *sound* kind to me. It may be in part because the poem has made clear how dearly Smith needs to be cherished—clear enough that it's easy to imagine the woman he's with would want to disappear into his delight in her. But it's also how Brooks writes here, the way her pleasure and mine seem to dim, not because these lines are less beautiful, but because they seem to take our pleasure less seriously. They seem gentle. The final "you," the one in "You get…," no longer means a reader. It's rhetorical now; almost something Smith might say. The inversion of that second-to-last stanza no longer flashes. The rhythm softens. The lines sway. They land at last, gently, on "home," which is in fact the apartment he left, where he bathed and dressed, where he shed his shabby days.

The vulnerability of those lines peers out intermittently throughout the poem, though it's rarely so sustained as in these final stanzas. "People are so in need," she writes early on, abruptly turning away from "our" inspection of his closet, "in need of help. / People want so much that they do not know." This sounds kind to me, too, though it seems almost to abandon Smith. The lines seem to be exasperated with "you"—with me—for a failure of imagination that is, in fact, a failure of kindness. "People." Both sentences start with that same word, and I can easily imagine an extra emphasis there, an insistence on humanity, an insistence that we see it. The first sentence stutters and restarts, trying to get it right. The second nearly falls apart grammatically, as if overwhelmed by the insufficiency of what it might say—"do not know" what? What they don't know? Where to start? The poem embodies, there, it's own sufficiency. And then the poem goes on.

When that exasperation next juts out, just a few stanzas after "People are so in need…," its frustration is even more pronounced. It comes at the end of the stanza that starts a little bit more simply, gearing down from the elaborate closing of a couplet, "The technique of a variegated grace."

> Here is all his sculpture and his art
> And all his architectural design.
> Perhaps you would prefer to this a fine
> Value of marble, complicated stone.
> Would have him think with horror of baroque,
> Rococo. You forget and you forget.

Here again the sentence falters poignantly, registering the excess of meaning it regards: "You forget and you forget." The things that I forget—some of them—she will begin to describe later on, but for now the scale of that forgetting is insurmountable. Reading that sentence, I'm unable to draw any line between anger and sorrow. She sounds almost like a parent who has run out of everything—patience, ideas, room—or a partner who has nothing left to give. And yet she hasn't really run out. Her exasperation and outrage here—no direct object, the conjunction that suggests addition but can't get her past her dismay, the repetition that could just as easily go on—are, unmistakably, the other side of her determination to care for Smith.

The sound of the poem changes after that. Brooks won't refer to "you" again until just before she shifts, in those last three stanzas, to the mode that seems almost to speak for Smith. And by then, "you" will seem largely irrelevant, the final address no more dramatic than pulling the keys from the door, having already turned the lock: "you" don't matter because you don't matter to Smith.

A few more lines, these a little later in the poem, a few long stanzas before "At Joes Eats…":

> Down these sore avenues
> Comes no Saint-Saëns, no piquant elusive Grieg,
> And not Tchaikovsky's wayward eloquence
> And not the shapely tender drift of Brahms.
> But could he love them? Since a man must bring
> To music what his mother spanked him for
> When he was two: bits of forgotten hate,
> Devotion: whether or not his mattress hurts:
> The little dream his father humored: the thing
> His sister did for money: what he ate
> For breakfast—and for dinner twenty years
> Ago last autumn: all his skipped desserts.

She doesn't answer the question—not explicitly—and she doesn't mention "you." It hardly matters now. The question yields entirely to his past, which she renders in lines that manage to be both intricate and imprecise. Smith's past yields to a host of pasts, a particularity of possibilities, all of them painful, all of them softened by the audible care of Brooks' litany. I hear that gentling, too, in the lines just before, as Brooks describes the things Smith "sees and does not see" while gliding through the neighborhood, the last of them "men estranged / From music and from wonder and from joy / But far familiar with the guiding awe / Of foodlessness." The tenderness of those lines, their plain availability to pain's almost-majestic presence in their lives, is inseparable from their confidence, their metered, sure-footed declaration of the terms of despair. Their poise. How the overt music in her list of the things from which they are estranged dissolves into the syntactical complexity of the next line, and how that lands, the "awe" lands, on the plain dry term for something almost unbearable, "Of foodlessness."

Why do lines like these sound so kind to me? And why do these, even closer to the end, which entail Brooks' final address to "you"?:

> Her affable extremes are like sweet bombs
> About him, whom no middle grace or good
> Could gratify. He had no education
> In quiet arts of compromise. He would
> Not understand your counsels on control, nor
> Thank you for your late trouble.

Especially in this poem, which navigates my presence so deftly and directly, I worry that my own appetites—which have nothing to do with foodlessness, nothing to do with any of the despairs that Smith transforms—seem to be sated by certain sounds. I worry that I'm mistaking something I need to hear for kindness. I worry about the "you" I bring into this poem, which is not the one that judges Smith but one that ends up using Brooks' use of him to heal myself.

But to decline the gifts the poem offers does nothing for the poem, and the poem does sound kind to me in ways that I think have to do with more than what is broken in me. The confidence of those lines seems to be based in a knowledge—knowledge, not hope or argument or belief— that Smith is central, important, worthy of not only Brooks' regard but of mine, whoever I might be. Brooks' dismissal of "you" feels effortless. It knows—at last, after the earlier arguments, it knows—that whatever need "you" have to feel good about your condescending kindness towards Smith is of no importance. And even as the poem will go on talking in terms that would be of no interest to Smith, it refuses the terms that would make him eccentric. It refuses his estrangement, taking seriously the pleasures that he has made into, against those estrangements, a life. "…like sweet bombs" she writes, and the poem does not explode. The poem, now, is sweet. It patiently makes his pleasure known. It sounds, however provisionally, at peace in ways that Smith might also, sometimes, provisionally, be.

"All We Can Say":
On Politics

If politics is, or was, or was rumored to be, the art of compromise, political poetry, as we typically understand it, is not. Political poetry is more often poetry of protest, meant to scald or cauterize, to rally or refuse. It aims away from the middle, toward the ideal, more likely to rally the base than to move the needle, to borrow a couple clichés from the politics of elections, strategists, and cable news.

The poetry of protest matters. It can embody the woundedness of those whose oppression is doubled by its exclusion from our more recognized forms of political discourse. It can offer energy to and enlarge the imagination of those who are working to change the world, as well as potentially encouraging more to do the same. It can be a place to think more clearly and richly about the things we already think about, and it can awaken those of us who are only half asleep to the injustices it describes.

But political poetry in America—American poetry at large, in its foregone marginalization and its presumed commitment to truth above practicality—rarely engages in what we most often mean when we mention "politics" outside of art. We rarely write or read poems that engage, strategically, with an audience that is persuadable but uncertain about the issue at hand, that treats those who might disagree as potential allies. A poetry of coalition building: How would *that* sound? And what value would it have? How would it reach those who aren't already in agreement? And would we accept it if it did?

Barack Obama left office as the most effective presidential champion of LGBTQ rights in American history (an admittedly low bar). And if his achievements in that regard were insufficient to what actual justice demands, it seems likely that he did most of what was politically possible at that moment in history. He entered office, on the other hand, as a familiar disappointment on the subject—championing civil unions rather than marriage equality, doing and saying too little for too long. It was only after an "evolution" that his work toward justice started. Whether that "evolution" reflected an actual change of mind or simply a withholding of his actual convictions until the electorate at large had shifted (and Vice President Biden had forced his hand), it's hard to imagine that he would have been elected in 2008 had he openly supported full marriage equality or legal protection for transgender and transsexual Americans.

It's hard to conceive of an American poet making a similarly strategic "evolution." That's not how we conceptualize poetry. The political center of American poetry is far to the left of the country at large, and so pitching a poem to an audience of American centrists would likely mean seeking an audience that hardly reads poems in the first place. And the allowance for expediency that some of us grant to politicians would never cross our minds in relationship to a poem. Sure, we understand a separation between speaker and poet, but not so much between poem and poet. A poem that strategically concedes some corner of justice in exchange for the more immediately achievable would be condemned as a moral failure.

If you've been paying attention to American poetry for the past half-decade or so, you're already familiar with Tony Hoagland's poem "The Change"—or, if not with the poem, at least with the argument about it that Claudia Rankine described in her 2011 speech at the AWP conference. The most notable part of that argument (I'm assuming Rankine's report is accurate since Hoagland, to borrow another political cliché, neither confirmed nor denied it in his public response) was Hoagland's explanation that the poem was or is "for white people." In the kindest possible interpretations, that's an awful choice of words. "For white people" conjures Jim Crow, "separate but equal," housing, education, jobs, a world of services and opportunities so meticulously parsed by race that even the water fountain must say "whites only."

But the moment interests me because it makes it possible to imagine a different moment, one in which the poem didn't end by suggesting that racism is "past us." One in which the author of the poem didn't say that the poem was "for white people" but instead said and meant "This poem is my attempt to seduce other white people into thinking about the ways racism still guides how we think." What if that kind of poetry—poetry aimed strategically, maybe even welcomingly, at an audience not already on its side, in the interest of moving that audience toward the work of justice not yet done—what if that kind of poetry were something we made, and something we embraced?

As it happens, Rankine is one of the very few "political" poets I can think of who does something similar to that—focusing on her poetry's implications for an audience not already in sympathy with her claims. *Citizen* does substantial work to pose her readers inside black bodies, so they must either experience racism from the perspective of a black person—or consciously refuse that experience. It's a book, especially in its first sections, that does substantial work to engage an audience that has never felt what it's like to live inside the erasures of a racist society.

I don't know of any successful American poems that are purely political in the sense that a political speech is. But I do think that there are recent poems that, like *Citizen*, incorporate such strategic choices into the more familiar forms of political poetry, sometimes drawing additional poetic value from the uneasy interplay between the two—and sometimes revealing something about the enduring difficulty of speaking across our political identities.

⌁

Perhaps uniquely among American poets, Jericho Brown comes out of the world of conventional politics; he once worked as a speechwriter for the mayor of New Orleans. His poem "Bullet Points" takes the form of a note to be read if he is ever killed by police (Brown is black), an attempt to preempt the usual explanations that are given when a black or brown man or woman dies in police custody or during an encounter with the police. The opening lines have the cadence and clarity of a public speech, as if anticipating the nature of the discussions that he will have been excluded from by the time such a note would be of use. The first line sounds complete: "I will not shoot myself." But across that first line ending, the statement becomes more specific, "I will not shoot myself / In the head," and with that specificity the poem enters the universe of ways in which a black or brown man or woman may be said by the police to have caused his or her own death:

> I will not shoot myself
> In the head, and I will not shoot myself
> In the back, I will not hang myself
> With a trashbag, and if I do,
> I promise you, I will not do it
> In a police car while handcuffed,
> Or in the jail cell of a town
> I only know the name of
> Because I have to drive through it
> To get home.

The structure here underscores the rhetoric. The first three line endings cause the second, third, and fourth lines to land hard on the specific ways in which he will not kill himself. Something similar happens in the shift from line five to six, but the last specification is longer and more detailed than the first three, so that you begin to hear the explanations growing more complex and even less conceivable, the addition of detail adding to the sense of Brown's outrage, the implausibility that someone even could kill himself this way.

In the seventh line, that momentum spills over. Instead

of resetting again by going back to the phrase "I will not," the poem picks up on the last part of the preceding sentence, the prepositional phrase that gives the location, "in…." You can hear the rhetorical structure now straining to hold the energy it's built. And you can hear, too, the poem's rhetoric becoming a little less careful, a little less strategic. The first six lines are narrowly tailored to articulate the number and improbability of the ways in which African Americans have been accused of killing themselves when killed by someone else. The mention of the "town," on the other hand, feels fed up—with all the ways he might be killed and with being so careful in how he speaks, as well. There's a note of "I didn't even want to be in this shitty town" to it that sounds less careful, less able to keep up the restraint of sticking to just one issue, of making no unnecessary enemies along the way. There's a shift, to put it differently, in the poem's apparent purpose, a move from political speech to speech act that manifests the outrage in more personal terms.

The poem pulls back momentarily, then: "Yes," he writes, appearing to concede a point, "I may be at risk." He's coming back to rhetoric, acknowledging a possible counterargument in order to tame and turn it to his purposes. The "Yes" implies an audience, an opponent, someone trying to point out a flaw in his argument—or, more accurately, a hole in an argument he hasn't made. That's how these debates work. When an officer shoots Walter Scott or an officer shoots Tamir Rice or Sandra Bland is found dead in a jail cell or Jesus Huerta, here in Durham, NC, is said to have shot himself while handcuffed in the backseat of a police car with a gun whose very presence in the backseat with him the officers can't explain, someone (many someones, in fact) will point out that violent crime is more common in black and brown neighborhoods—an act of blaming the victim that also erases the individuality of the victim, making him or her a representative of the neighborhood, and the neighborhood a representative of crime.

Brown tries to preempt that claim by accepting it, to avoid

its use as a distraction from his having been murdered. When dead, he won't be able to say anything, and so he has to anticipate it all now, which makes the poem an image of all the ways in which a black or brown person might be erased under the cover of policing—or, rather, of the impossibility of accounting for them all. The poem's posture has failure built into it. That sense of insufficiency, of being fed up, spills over from the first, long, accelerating sentence through the brief attempt to get back to strategic public discourse ("yes") to the next sentence, where the impatience of even having to stop and acknowledge such a thing flares up into anger, and Brown begins marshaling his ingenuity toward insult, the genius for wounding we have when we're especially hurt. He's done with trying to seek consensus from those who won't meet him here; the poem is about to turn into a record of, among other things, how much it hurts, how infuriating it is, to try.

When we discussed this poem on our short-lived podcast, francine j. harris spoke of the next sentence ("Yes, I may be at risk, / But I promise you, I trust the maggots / And the ants and the roaches / Who live beneath the floorboards / Of my house to do what they must / To any carcass than I trust / An officer of the law of the land / To shut my eyes like a man / Of God might...."), in terms of "a desire not to let violence be the thing that picks you apart, to let the earth be the thing that picks you apart." I think she's right, but I also hear a sharp insult, maggots and roaches, the lowest of the low: "beneath my floorboards," with the "my" maybe serving as a small reminder that he's a property owner, someone who has earned his place in the American Dream. He trusts them, he says, the maggots and ants and roaches, more than he trusts any officer to treat his dead body with respect. For anyone who enters the poem with a belief that most officers are well-meaning, that the law and its agents are worthy of respect, that these killings, while troubling, are still exceptional, this is not the sort of declaration that will invite consent. It's the sort of thing that sends people running back to their assumptions, doubling down on what they think they already know.

From that point on, the poem never fully returns to the more narrowly constructed arguments of its first sentences. The patience required for such a thing—for an approach that invites in and accommodates those who want to believe in the fundamental goodness of America writ large—ends up feeling unsustainable. The poem's seductions, henceforth, have to do with wit and beauty.

> When I kill me, I will kill me
> The same way most Americans do
> I promise you: cigarette smoke,
> Or a piece of meat on which I choke,
> Or so broke I freeze
> In one of those winters we keep
> Calling worst.

Like the earlier "Yes," "I promise you" implies an audience, but no longer the same one. It sounds more personal now, as if the point is less to persuade the country at large than to provide some comfort to those who will lose him. A few lines later he writes, in the past tense (all this so inevitable it's already happened now), "He took / Me from us." As the rhymes pile up and the syntax grows more formal, the image of America gets increasingly scornful, the gluttonous citizen choking on a piece of meat, the endemic poverty, the determined blindness to climate change. He's off-topic now, too tired of it all to be polite, ready to tell America what he really thinks of it. He's also reminding us that none of this is exceptional, that police don't kill black and brown people because a few bad apples are racist, or because the police are themselves some island of racism in an otherwise just country, but that these murders root and tangle in every part of American life.

The poem ends up far from hope, the speaker already dead, the government action (another payout) of no consequence, trying once again to declare his value, too late, his body, left behind, still beautiful, "more / Beautiful than the brand new shiny bullet / Fished from the folds of my brain." After the dense stresses of "brand new shiny bullet," the last line opens up, an anapestic trimester stretching out into song, the alliteration of "fished" and "folds" emphasizing the almost-languorous rhythm, the brain just brain but beautiful, too, now that it's been revealed, but mindless, the site of a pointless forensic fishing expedition, getting the bullet that will show none of the reasons he was killed.

≈

If a poem were to speak to an audience of people at the center of American politics, it would have to find them first, and the most common crossover space for poems is social media, where the rare poem achieves escape velocity, entering the feeds of poets' family and friends. Matthew Olzmann's "Letter Beginning with Two Lines by Czesław Miłosz" did that. First emailed out as part of the Academy of American Poets' "Poem a Day" program, the poem went far fast, an emblem for Americans fed up with our inability to even diminish the availability of guns.

The poem begins, after the Miłosz lines, by inviting consensus: "Can we agree Kevlar / backpacks shouldn't be needed // for children walking to school?" The poem constructs the largest possible "we" in that moment, offering an image so absurd that no one would dare disagree. Yes. We can agree. But in being so open to everyone, the poem also takes a risk of being put to other uses. It's easy enough to imagine someone using that image to argue, for instance, that welfare has corrupted American cities, or that the supposed breakdown of black families has led to a derangement of American society, or that the loss of Christian authority has done that, or all three.

"Letter" doesn't actually invite those interpretations. Maybe because of context, maybe because of tone, maybe because it seems to be arguing, implicitly, already, for a place where no bullets are in the air, it's clear in these early consensus-seeking moments that Olzmann isn't advocating, for example, more guns. But for the same reasons I can imagine someone putting these first materials in Olzmann's argument to very different use, I wonder if the poem's popularity comes not only from its very real power but also from that fact that such power, much like a gun, remains available to a variety of uses. I'll come back to that later on.

The poem has covered more than 25 lines before it says anything potentially disagreeable. It constructs an enemy we can all agree on: murder. It appeals to our feelings for the most sacred of citizens—children. It puts them inside our most privileged of spaces—their homes, their yards and then, since property and commerce are sacred to some, too, a restaurant where they've purchased food. In doing so, it isolates them from the terms of such appalling dismissals as *What was he doing there in the first place? Her parents should have…*. Yes. We can agree. But there's no escaping the sense that we're being set up, our consent secured in the interest of some other, potentially less agreeable argument. And so when Olzmann ends a line and starts a sentence with the word "But," it seems we're about to enter that argument. The poem already seems by then to be drifting into something darker, plainer, truer: "They"—the children—"shouldn't have to stop // to consider the speed / of a bullet or how it might // reshape their bodies." The images of gun violence shed their exaggeration there. No longer the protective snipers in McDonald's, it's now the child's imagination of a real bullet passing through his or her real flesh. "But…."

"But / one winter, back in Detroit, // I had one student / who opened a door and died." One winter, one student. The "but" doesn't yet open into argument. It just means that we do live in that world. It means that this is the real world, that children would need armor just to stand safely in their yards, that death arrives so fast in the form of a bullet that merely letting in the outside air admits enough space to eliminate a child. That this is singular and personal. That we are already there—that we are here. (Or, at least, we're in Detroit. But the poem doesn't say why that matters, and we're left to wonder, depending on who and where we are, how much this poem is about us, beyond our agreement, of course. We're left to think about what we think about "Detroit," which probably depends in part on who we are and where we live.) And the verb, the avoidance of passive voice; not "was shot," not "was hit by a stray bullet," not "was murdered," not "was killed." Instead, the syntax makes the student into the actor, erasing, distressingly, the gun, the bullet, the shooter. There are two parallel actions: the student opened the door, the student died. You can almost hear the logic of "guns don't kill people; people do," a line Olzmann will invoke later in the poem, going to its logical extreme—no cause, all effect: "who opened a door and died."

Moving into that reality changes the poem's tone. The anger is harder to ignore, and a kind of urgency slips in, the phrases getting shorter and blunter now. Olzmann seems desperate to keep his readers from looking away, from writing the student off. Instead of making the student specific, he insists that the student could have been any student, any child. If the student lived in poverty, he doesn't say. If the student was black or brown, he doesn't say. And while it's of course possible that the student wasn't poor or of color, it's also true that people in poverty and people of color are disproportionately harmed by the easy availability of guns in this country, and it's also possible that those details—from Detroit, where roughly 80% of citizens are black and almost 40% live below the poverty line—don't make it into the poem because details like those would make it too easy for many readers to stop imagining their own child opening that door. "It was the front / door to his house, but" (once again, the "but" comes at the end of a line) "it could have been any door,

/ and the bullet could have written // any name." Later in the poem, he'll push further out, into the kinds of killings that seem to gather more of our attention, that happen more often in suburbs, to white people, on the news: "Today, / there's another // shooting with dead / kids everywhere. It was a school, // a movie theater, a parking lot."

Olzmann is back in the universalizing rhetoric here, but it's more charged now, less *can we all agree on this* than *you can't keep ignoring this*. It's escalating now, picking up speed. For a third time, the turn comes at the end of the line, with the word "but," and if you listen closely you can hear the echo of someone arguing with someone else who will not yield: "but…, but…, but…."

But

> a bullet doesn't care
> about "aim," it doesn't
>
> distinguish between
> the innocent and the innocent,
>
> and how was the bullet
> supposed to know this
>
> child would open the door
> at the exact wrong moment
>
> because his friend
> was outside and screaming
>
> for help. Did I say
> I had "one" student who
>
> opened a door and died?
> That's wrong.
>
> There were many.

The two lines from Miłosz that the poem starts with, "You whom I could not save, / Listen to me," make it hard to tell, at first, who he's talking to. The people Olzmann seems not to have saved are, most obviously, the people killed by guns. But he's not talking to them in this poem. He's talking to us— some vast American "we." And so the "you" he could not save (it's already, apparently, too late) is us, America, unable to stop killing ourselves. Near the end of the poem he circles back: "And you, whom I cannot save, // you may open a door // and enter a meadow, or a eulogy." The alternatives there, the meadow or the eulogy, suggest something of the country's broken self-image—the pastoral and the violent a kind of binary—and the implication that either one could be on the other side of the door for "you" attempts to stitch them together, to stitch us together in the belief that any of us could be the victim. It's noteworthy here that Milosz's "could not" has shifted to "cannot"—the impossibility a little fresher now, the aspiration to save us less remote.

By then the poem is slowing down. Almost thirty lines have passed since "There were many," and now it feels like he's run out of hope of convincing us to do something. The poem becomes elegiac, even as it prepares to condemn our eulogizing. It's a bitter elegy, an elegy for the "you" who refuses an easily available cure. The poem doesn't say what that cure is. It mimics our asking, mocking our performance of innocence. The "latter" here refers to opening a door and entering a eulogy:

And if the latter, you will be

mourned, then buried
in rhetoric.

There will be
monuments of legislation,

little flowers made
from red tape.

What should we do? we'll ask
again. The earth will close

like a door above you.
What should we do?

And that click you hear?
That's just our voices,

the deadbolt of discourse
sliding into place.

Here at the end, the poem sneers at rhetoric, at language, discourse (and of course, it does all of this in language, rhetoric…), treating it as the thing we offer instead of action. The door that the student opened and died, that later became the point of entry to meadow or eulogy, is now the earth itself above the grave, the earth itself rhetoric, and discourse seals it closed. The metaphor gets a little wobbly. What, for example, is the difference between rhetoric and the discourse that latches it shut? And what about these lines: "There will be / monuments of legislation, // little flowers made / from red tape." Legislation seems like another meaningless response— another thing that will not save us. And so, it's worth asking, what does this poem, this rhetorical device that has no faith in rhetoric, hope to make of our agreement?

And so it seems worth asking what we (I was among those who shared it on Facebook) were doing when we pushed the poem a little further out into the world. Neither the poem nor I offered anything we might agree on, any legislation or other action we could push for or engage in. And I wonder if that wasn't among the reasons we were so quick to carry this poem out into the world, if it's vision of powerless outrage didn't lend itself to the self-presentation that is so much a part of our lives online—the long-cultivated image of ourselves that is drawn in large part in opposition, our identities safest when they are based on who we are not.

I don't say that to disparage "Letter." There's far more to Olzmann's poem than that. But it's striking to think about the poem's "we," which returns at the end: "our voices." The "you" ("that click you hear") seems to still be a version of us, or a part of us at least, the part that opened the door to a eulogy. And the "we," to whatever extent it's still possible to imagine a "we" at this point of the poem, is drawn together not by consent but by failure. What we have in common, the poem suggests, is not anything we might agree on but rather that we haven't saved anyone from this.

≈

That very word "we" lies awkwardly across the American grain; it has tended to erase at least as much as it includes. In Sterling Brown's 1938 poem "Southern Cop," a "we" speaks with blunt certainty about an unnamed person who is referred to throughout as "the Negro" and the *named* white police officer who shot him: Ty Kendricks, who is often referred to, familiarly, as "Ty"—almost, but not quite, one of us. "Ty" is also sometimes "he." "The Negro" never is.

The poem stands at the other end of the attempted dialogue of Jericho Brown's "Bullet Points," creating a voice for those who would refuse to weigh the destruction of a black life against the fears and vulnerabilities of the man who killed him. It's a reminder, from 80 years earlier, of all the reasons "Bullet Points" would struggle to persuade, no matter how narrowly he tailored his argument. The terms of dismissal are too old, entrenched and rehearsed—and for many too obviously true.

The speakers of "Southern Cop" (or, it may be, one speaker gathering others into these shared understandings) are working toward compassion. The murder they justify is, for them, incidental. They are, by their lights, trying to bring kindness to someone in need of support, and it would likely shock them to hear someone thought their response anything other than generous. Kendricks seems to be a lesser member of society, and a note of polite condescension runs throughout the poem; they have already bent down so far. And so even within the bounds of whiteness, it's possible to hear the limits of the "we" at work in the poem, and to hear in that how any extension of the privileges of whiteness must both invoke and erase a non-white presence that draws the perimeters by threatening them.

Sterling isn't interested in these people as complex characters, but rather in their identity as a functioning collective. After a first stanza in which a series of uncomfortably short declarative sentences assemble like an argument, leading to the final, two-beat line, with its pretenses of a logical conclusion and its arrival at the poem's first rhyme—"And so he shot"—the poem's rhetoric begins to crack. As the "we" works to sweep this or that ash of reality under the carpet, it exposes itself to the poem's readers (though not to itself). The second stanza, with its goal of understanding Kendricks, seems to understand him all too well:

> Let us understand Ty Kendricks.
> The Negro must have been dangerous,
> Because he ran;
> And here was a rookie with a chance
> To prove himself a man.

The cracks in their logic *are* their logic, and the sickening power of "Southern Cop" sparks in that implausible fusion, the logic built of illogic much as the "we" is built of exclusion.

"The Negro" becomes more prominent as the poem goes on. In the third and penultimate stanza—in which the speakers condone Kendricks since they "cannot decorate"—he gets two mentions, though in neither case is he the subject of the sentence:

> When he found what the Negro was running for,
> It was too late;
> And all we can say for the Negro is
> It was unfortunate.

Their case is appalling—that's the point. And the longer they speak, the worse it gets, the more glaring and prominent and almost explicit what they're not saying becomes. That's the point, too—to inhabit this language in order to expose it, to let it expose itself. "Unfortunate" rhymes weakly against "late," accentuating the word's absurd insufficiency, its diminishment of both the devastation caused and the actions that caused it— relegating them to the realm of fortune, which is beyond human action or help. And "All we can say" is flatly untrue, even within the boundaries of this stanza. Strikingly, the one strategy they don't engage in is that of claiming that "the Negro" was guilty. In a world where "unfortunate" might seem sufficient, there's no apparent need for that.

The final stanza advocates "pity" and then foregrounds the pity denied. The language here gets richer, and in the final line the epithet for "the Negro" for the first and last time takes on an added term, as he becomes more specific and more audibly afflicted:

> Let us pity Ty Kendricks.
> He has been through enough,
> Standing there, his big gun smoking,
> Rabbit-scared, alone,
> Having to hear the wenches wail
> And the dying Negro moan.

"Rabbit-scared," "the wenches wail," "the dying Negro moan": the writing here is more figurative, more cruel, and more musical. More full of life and more full of the capacity to kill. Even as "the wenches" introduces an insult that's new to the speakers' polite poise (and, maybe not coincidentally, introduces women into the poem for the first time, too), and even as they're framed as something that the pitied and perhaps a little stupid Kendricks would have to hear, they also contrast with the "alone"ness of Kendricks, a reminder that "the Negro" was part of a community, a "we" that is utterly outside the "we" of the poem and is granted no language, just wailing and moaning (the latter rhyming pointedly with "alone").

The poem ends with a terrible sense of resolution, but it also spirals out into greater levels of complexity. In including his "Having to hear the wenches wail / And the dying Negro moan" among the hardships Kendricks has already suffered, the speakers admit to the reality of "the Negro" and "the wenches" as people who suffer, and whose suffering has reality enough to cause empathetic pain of the very kind they refuse throughout the poem. They acknowledge this as something more than unfortunate, even as they use that to minimize the need to punish Kendricks for causing it. They introduce the idea of his guilt in saying that he has already suffered enough. And they push Kendricks outside of the circle understanding might and decorating certainly would have brought him into. They have, that is to say, made him singular; they have singled him out. And if they cannot—or, in their misplaced benevolence, in their theater of generosity, will not—condemn him, neither can they pull him too close.

Brown gives his last word to the wordless dying man. The moan, once again grammatically subordinate, is the poem's final and most memorable element. For most readers, and maybe (though only maybe) even for some of the speakers, it haunts both the poem that precedes it and the silence that comes after. It is a reminder that if we (and by "we" here I mean especially people like me, white people) are to speak credibly about any kind of American "we," we will have to do so in a way that can accommodate that moan and the millions of other moans that have been omitted from American discourse for all the centuries of its being.

≈

The idea of an authorized American "we" is often predicated on treating a privileged norm as a universal standard, and so the use of "I" has often been a first step toward correcting the record, asserting the authority of a voice that the "we" would exclude. As in so many of her poems, in "if i stand in my window" Lucille Clifton places her black, female body, with all its historical implications, but also with its immediate reality, at the center of her singing. The poem, which is a single continuous if/then statement, begins in delight and never departs. Each of the first three lines includes the word 'my,' and in the second line she pairs it with 'own,' grounding the poem's assertions in ownership, something most African Americans couldn't claim over even their own flesh for centuries, nor—for most—over land or housing for well over a century after that:

> if i stand in my window
> naked in my own house
> and press my breasts
> against the windowpane
> like black birds pushing against glass

After a second "if" ("if the man come to stop me / in my own house") she conjures "the man"'s response in a final stanza that begins not with "then" but with "let him"—a lordly condescension reminiscent of the "Let us" in "Southern Cop":

> let him watch my black body
> push against my own glass
> let him discover self
> let him run naked through the streets
> crying
> praying in tongues

The poem does not refuse a white audience. What it rejects—what it revels in its power to reject—is "the man"'s attempt to make her answerable to his taking offense. It declares her house and her poem as a place of almost magical immunity to that judgment, her body so powerful that "the man" will not only end up naked himself, out in "the streets / crying / praying in tongues," but will also "discover self," come into contact with his own singularity, no longer "the man" in any collective sense but simply an individual without any special authority.

The poem is a fantasy, too. But that fantasy creates a needed reality, even if "the man" will not, in fact, discover anything. For that to happen, for "the man" to "discover self," he would first have to feel that his self were safe. And that's not what the poem is here for, any more than "Bullet Points" ultimately is, perhaps in part because that—that feeling of safety for a man, "*the* man," who feels so threatened by the body he spies on—seems not only impossible but unimaginable here.

If we do want to persuade those who disagree with us, who see themselves as not being "us" in the first place, then before asking the question "Can we agree?" we may first have to answer the question "Can I trust you?" The whole idea of this appalls many, and understandably so, especially if you're among those still being kicked around and even killed by the man. But I do believe it's possible, without asking those who are aggrieved to do the work of conciliation and without losing our sense of proportion, to recognize that most of us are wounded, including those who wound. And even as I doubt poetry has the influence to alter American political life, I do believe that it offers models of imagination and interaction, of what we can say, and how, and how we can be addressed. To that end, Clifton's 1991 poem "won't you celebrate with me" seems especially significant. The "you" that it invokes, like Rankine's, is likely to alter in meaning depending on who reads it, but here it's an identity any reader could enter without forsaking his or her own self-conception. The poem introduces "you" even before it mentions the speaker. And unlike Olzmann's "Can we agree," the opening sentence gives no suggestion of having a design on its reader beyond its welcome:

> won't you celebrate with me
> what i have shaped into
> a kind of life? i had no model.

The phrase "a kind of life," though, runs askance from the idea of celebration. It suggests something imperfect—"kind of" implying not that this is one kind among the many available but that this is only sort of a life. The small sentence that follows seems to apologize for that shortcoming, or at least to explain it. But as she does, continuing her explanation, that same insufficiency turns out to be the reason for celebration—a recognition of its achievement, its artifice, and its integrity, based in the encounter with herself:

> born in babylon
> both nonwhite and woman
> what did i see to be except myself?
> i made it up...

It is, from one angle, easy to see this as a claim of self-reliance, a rejection of the poets, traditions, and pioneers that preceded her, as well as the community of friends and family that helped her to grow. She describes the creation as occurring with "my one hand holding tight / my other hand." But even as she claims that she worked without models, she builds the poem on a series of allusions. More pronounced and more persuasive is Clifton's attempt to make an active and improvisatory community inclusive of anyone willing to accept her invitation.

The poem's concluding sentence—"come celebrate / with me that everyday / something has tried to kill me / and has failed"—introduces an outside force against which the community might define itself: "something." It's a vague term, made real by the menace she attributes to it and the easy confidence with which she does so. Like "the man" in "if I stand in my window," it's an artfully constructed enemy, both imprecise and persuasive, and yet as in that poem, Clifton seems to pull no punches. Among the reasons "something" has tried to kill her is that she is, "both nonwhite and woman," and the attempt to kill her continues to happen "everyday."

It's also a funny sentence—however darkly. Before that final line, the poem seems to ask its readers to celebrate "that everyday / something has tried to kill me." The final line reverses that, but it doesn't remove it. The celebration isn't just rooted in the fact that she's alive; it's rooted in all that she has survived. Among the things that distinguish Clifton from most other important American poets is the radiant health of her poems. Even when she writes on illness, she seems to stand effortlessly, healthily, in her knowledge of the world as it is, however unforgivable what she sees. It's what makes her such a healing presence in American literature, someone who can balance awareness and even embodiment of the moan that ends Brown's "Southern Cop" and an impulse to live fully and compassionately. Whether or not anyone who isn't already interested in listening to the implications of that moan will accept Clifton's invitation, will ever become the kind of person the poem could meaningfully invite, I can't say with any confidence. But if we won't, I fear that we (that the hope, even, of a meaningful American "we") are too wounded, too warped by our attempts to live outside our history and by our blindness and rage, to heal or progress anytime soon.

～

Most of the poets I've written about in this chapter are black. None of them are white. I am. I want to be clear: it's not the responsibility of those who have been and continue to be most harmed by the history of American privilege to reach out. Rather, I think that those on whose bodies our politics have been most deeply and persistently inscribed have often written most profoundly of the erasures that our failures of imagination (the failures, that is, of people like me), our failures to speak meaningfully, comprehensively, when we say "we," have written into the world, and of the cost of writing so much, and so many, out of view.

Nor do I mean to say that the poetry of protest is less valuable than the poetry (were it to exist) of consensus-building. What I want to say is, I think, after all these words, something smaller, wider, and possibly more naïve than that.

In "The Sundays of Satin Legs Smith," Gwendolyn Brooks takes leave, momentarily, of the rich language that relishes Smith's gaudy wardrobe to state, plainly, "People are so in need, in need of help. / People want so much that they do not know." She's writing of black people in a black neighborhood in the 1940s, and I'm wary of uprooting these lines to speak of something broader than that. And yet: they are. They do. Our anger is (our angers are?) so pronounced right now, so present and bent, so dry and sere. It's easy and it's accurate to put a lot of this down to bigotry. But it's also true that people are so in need, in need of help. That people want so much that they do not know. Part of what they want is to be heard, even if they, even if we, don't know what we want to say. I do not think that poems can cure us. They play too small a part in American life. But we write them anyway, and we read them anyway, and sometimes they can show us something about what it takes to hear each other, to be vulnerable and broken and to be beautiful still. Sometimes even in the style of their speech they can show us what it might sound like to hear.

Poems won't save us. On the worst days, and there have been many of them recently, I'm not sure anything will. And yet some things go on improving, too. And some of us are angry about that. Can we agree? Can we even say "we" without leaving someone out? Probably not. Especially after the election of a president who based his appeal on the presentation of explicit bigotry as a kind of intellectual freedom and integrity, it's hard to imagine in the present tense's plausible future. And yet the ideal of a functional, vibrant, encompassing "we" remains essential, as do aesthetic acts that measure both the pull of that ideal and the cost of our failure.

"The Goal of Jokes": On Humor

Humor is at once, potentially, remarkably intimate (to make someone laugh is to override, at least momentarily, that person's bodily control) and, among those features that define our social lives, unusually broad. It's often impersonal, frequently invested in collective knowledge or assumptions, frequently tangled in the social categories—race, gender, sexuality, religion, class—that unite and divide us, depending on who we mean by "we." It can depend entirely on the moment in which it occurs ("you had to be there," we explain later on) or the people who share it, but it's also one of the few parts of our social life where working from a script doesn't seem out of place. We accept a level of performance from our friends when they try to make us laugh that would seem self-centered if humor weren't the goal.

Poems, especially short ones, are natural joke-tellers. Think of rhyme as a kind of call back. Think of the volta as the start of a punch-line. Think of how much most jokes depend on expectation, which is what the patterns of traditional poems, in particular—meter, line-length, rhyme—set up.

Poems are best, it seems to me, at dark humor. Something about the bite. Maybe something about it being written down in something other than a joke book, something about what I've gotten used to thinking poems are—things to reread, to consider, things that still feel alive once the surprise is over, that can go on speaking in the same voice, to the same audience. Darkness keeps the impulse of their speech alive—beyond humor—as in Amiri Baraka's "Low Coup" poems, including "In the Funk World":

> If Elvis Presley is King
> Who is James Brown?
> God!?!

or, a little longer and a lot more severe, "Culture"

european jews
say the devil
speak perfect
german

black
americans on
the other
hand, say he
speak pretty
good english
too!

But these poems aren't really social in nature, which may
be one of the reasons I like them. Humor in poems tends
to remind me how much poems differ from our social life.
The poems that really present themselves as social acts, as
interactions—those genial, well-meaning poems that intend
to be funny and friendly—usually leave me cold. I don't want
to make too much of that. Other people adore those same
poems. But I always feel as if they have a design on me. Of
course, pretty much all poems have a design on me (or on
you—on someone), but there's something about those poems
that seem to be lying about it, acting as if they just want me
to be happy when, it always feels to me, they're asking for my
approval. And, to be honest, I typically have that same reaction
to real people who seem to be trying for the same—a sense
of cloying in the constant performance. A sense that we're
supposed to pretend we're hanging out when I'm really being
treated as an audience, and that the person is evaluating my
work as an audience—that I owe it to them to laugh. In that
sense, I guess, such poems do capture some aspects of our
social lives, including the neuroses I bring to mine.

If a poem is going to put on a show, I'd much rather it be up
front about it and then put its energy into making the show as

effective as possible, and to stand or fall on its success in that mode. I'd much rather look at something like Allen Ginsberg's "America" or Lucille Clifton's "wishes for sons" and laugh or not, care or not, keep reading or not, with no bones about what we're doing.

⌐

But then again, what we're doing is rarely as simple as we think. Jill McDonough's "Breasts Like Martinis" is not, outside of a few lines, a funny poem, but it's both playful and pointed in its rendering of how jokes work. At the bar where McDonough and her partner Josey are hanging out, the bartender and another customer seem blind—or, if not blind, then indifferent—to the implications for others, including the two (at least) women there, of the old lines that their jokes re-entrench. McDonough and Josey mock the tired, familiar jokes ("I whisper / *Sarah Evers told me that joke in sixth grade*"), and after we have had a chance to figure out the problem isn't just that the jokes are old ("A whore, a midget, a Chinaman"),

> a customer asks
> *Why are breasts like martinis?* and they both start
>   laughing.
> They know this one, everybody knows this one, except
> us. They don't even bother with the punch line. The
>   bartender just says
> *Yeah, but I always said there should be a third one, on the*
>   *back,*
> *for dancing,* dancing with the woman-shaped air behind
>   the bar, his hand
> on the breast on her back. So we figure three is too many,
> one's not enough.

"They know this one, everybody knows this one, except / us." The way "they" opens out to "everyone" and "everyone" counters the "us" that lands hard, a lone syllable after the break; "everyone" pivots from "their" perspective to "ours," so you can hear it from both sides, both its ease and its isolation. It shifts the locus of power in the poem for a moment. After the couple's easy dismissal of the jokes, the loss of familiarity is also a loss of footing. You can feel a little bit of fear creep in, a little reminder of how vulnerable women's bodies are. But then McDonough and Josey take over the joke, making their own exclusive world, and the bartender and his customer disappear. The jokes carry them out of the bar, back into their lives, into the days, weeks, months to come, as it turns into an inside joke, and inside, where we, as readers are also allowed to go, the jokes get funny, if also, finally, dark, circling back to the menace that flared up, briefly, in the bar:

> Okay; we can do better than that. *I like my breasts like I like my martinis,* we say: *Small and bruised* or *big and dry. Perfect.*
> *Overflowing. Reeking of juniper, spilling all over the bar.*
> When I have a migraine and she reaches for me, I say
> *Josey, my breasts are like martinis.* She nods, solemn:
> *People should keep their goddamn hands off yours.*

The first word after "one's not enough" is a one-word sentence, "Okay," that seems to come from both of them. A moment to steady themselves and resume their advantage. Rather than offence, they respond with humor of their own— humor that they keep to themselves, that reiterates their belonging to each other, rather than their belonging in the bar, which only gets one more mention in the poem. That mention forecloses on the possibility of bringing the bartender into their conversation, an impulse McDonough only considers in the subjunctive, in a rhetorical question that she then goes on to answer, registering the weight of the impossibility in stating explicitly what the question already implied: "How / could we tell these jokes to the bartender? We can't. He'll never know."

There's an unexpected sadness in those two short sentences, pity for him, that he'll miss out on the greater humor of a better world—or maybe for themselves, that there is no safe place for their humor in a bar that was at least worth walking into and ordering a drink. There are only three more lines after that, two more jokes, but the pleasure has gone out of them. The understanding they have is an understanding of the vulnerability another's body can contain: "dirty and wet," "shaking, ice cold." We sometimes overstate, I think, the connection between humor and tragedy, though the connection is there. What's more notable here, I think, is the poem's ability to exemplify, in unfamiliar terms, the also-familiar notion that humor increases the bonds between those who share it while also defining a perimeter around them, beyond which others would be unwelcome, or invisible, or lost.

The parallel between the joke-telling in the bar at the beginning and the joke-telling within the relationship at the end is unavoidable. The parallel is not an equivalency, though. In deciding to write a poem about humor more than a humorous poem, McDonough also chooses an empathetic complexity that humor wouldn't allow. She instead achieves an articulate ambiguity, which allows the poem to register the different kinds of isolation people assuage with humor, including the harm done by some humor. It does not treat all assuaging as equal. It does not treat all drawing of lines as equal. But it does create, in part through its drawing of those lines, an imaginative space in which they can overlap without losing their distinction.

~

There's a wrinkle in this essay that I can't smooth out. I almost never like funny poems. They often just end up reminding me that poems aren't quite social: Maybe because they assume a sense of humor that isn't mine, and maybe because they depend on my responding in a certain way (being amused), they remind me more than most that their gestures toward an audience aren't actually toward me. (That I so rarely grate against that in other contexts is, of course, among other things, a mark of my privilege.) And humor in general, especially humor based in absurdity, which is a thick strand in American poetry, often depends on breaking down familiar categories, which I depend on to make a world that was, for much of my life, baffling and, by extension, frightening, more navigable. That the breakdown often seems like a means of creating a new set of categories—creating an air of superiority, mocking, tearing down—just reiterates, for me, the one clear point my confusion, first as a child and then as an adult still seeing the world through childish anxieties, always made clear: my insufficiency. That is, by and large, my problem, though—and problematic, too, since depending on categorical certainties is just a short walk, even on a good day, from investing in an entire arsenal of bigotries, the same bigotries much absurdist comedy mocks.

⌇

There is, though, a part of that strand that I prefer, one that generates humor by playing with expectations and stereotypes, but whose play depends less on a sense of being beyond—above—all that, on a sense that there's some higher plane free of categories, and instead seems to involve some vulnerability on the part of the author. It's sometimes the vulnerability of reaching toward a space where more meaningful distinctions might be possible, including, in some cases, making more legible their anger at a world in which the established categories that govern life are profoundly unjust. In others it's as simple as the vulnerability of being playful, of retaining an element of innocence, or of caring for someone else.

The gentle absurdity that rattles through Terrance Hayes's "Woofer (When I Consider the African American)" is inseparable from its attempt to chip loose something of value from the absurdity of its circumstances—particularly the means by which those circumstances are typically understood. The poem is streaked with affection and frequently given over to delight, and it's consistently satirical, as both the title and the opening sentence broadcast:

> When I consider the much discussed dilemma
> of the African-American, I think not of the diasporic
> middle passing, unchained, juke, jock, and jiving
> sons and daughters of what sleek dashikied poets
> and tether fisted Nationalists commonly call Mother
> Africa, but of an ex-girlfriend who was the child
> of a black-skinned Ghanaian beauty and Jewish-
> American, globetrotting ethnomusicologist.

With a characteristic combination of heavy rhythms and light touch, Hayes seems to be having fun. But that fun is also a kind of remove. The pleasure of a poem is sometimes less the felt connection to another than the opportunity to witness mastery beyond your own (my own) abilities. If our social lives most often depend on knowing and being known, our willingness to become an audience involves an expectation that we will, in exchange, see, hear, something extraordinary, and to encounter it as something both within in our grasp and beyond our control, as well as the promise that the experience is something we can then have in common with someone else.

Hayes's mastery manifests in his ability to move with such audible speed through such variety without ever falling into incoherence. And in this case, it's a run of collective identities, as well as ways of talking about them—the material of many jokes, as well as our uneasy American identity—that Hayes strings together even as he satirizes them. There is an underlying instability in the sentence, a sense that any kind of word, any kind of tone, might come next on the string. But that madcap mode also highlights the continuity it resists.

So it goes with humor: the mastery of materials that seem

to have other intentions. That's where the pleasure comes from. And since both poems and jokes are notoriously resistant to paraphrase, there's no better way to ruin the fun here than to try to pin Hayes down. It's nonetheless safe to say that Hayes's doesn't altogether reject the terms he claims not to think of—and enumerates at length in making that claim. That they are overblown aspirations toward nailing down an in-fact fluid identity is not completely separable here from the occasional self-seriousness that Hayes also works to head off in himself, nor from the terms he uses (also undermining them) to introduce the ex-girlfriend who still, it seems, amazes him, and whose comically rendered complexity is part of her appeal.

Hayes's poem makes a show of doubling back:

> I forgot all my father's warnings about meeting women
> at bus stops (which is the way he met my mother)
> when I met her waiting for the rush hour bus in
> October

and

> When I think of African-American rituals
> of love, I think not of young, made-up unwed mothers
> who seek warmth in the arms of any brother
> with arms because they never knew their fathers
> (though that could describe my mother)

It also stays a little slippery, at least until the final sentence, when the poem seems, surprisingly, to conclude with its own overarching image of African American identity:

> I think of a string of people connected one to another
> and including the two of us there in the basement
> linked by a hyphen filled with blood;
> linked by a blood filled baton in one great historical
> relay.

The last line calls back an earlier pun—"everyone / is a descendant of slaves (which makes me wonder / if outrunning your captors is not the real meaning of Race?)"—but that doesn't much alter the sense that Hayes is ending here with a statement that is exempt from the approach he has taken in the rest of the poem. It feels disappointingly neat, in spite of its inventiveness, in spite of the missing hyphen, "filled with blood" or not, in the phrase "blood filled" (another mark—or maybe it's better to call it an erasure—of Hayes' ingenuity, but not one that can be *heard* in the poem, not one that can enter its voice). This is where poems that use incongruity as a tool but do not intend actual absurdity often falter. Compare that ending to these lines, which follow "(though that could describe my mother)":

> but of that girl
> and me in the basement of her father's four story
>   Victorian
> making love among the fresh blood and axe
> and chicken feathers left after the Thanksgiving
>   slaughter
> executed by a 3-D witchdoctor houseguest (his face
> was starred by tribal markings) and her ruddy America
> poppa while drums drummed upstairs from his hi-fi
>   woofers
> because that's the closest I've ever come to anything
> remotely ritualistic or African, for that matter.

Movement animates these lines. Like the punch line of a good joke, they swerve in unexpected directions, even into the slight hint of wistfulness in the last two lines, except in this case, such swerving defines the set up; it's the constant the punch line will have to somehow reverse. And so at the end of this excerpt, the only remaining way to swerve is to stop swerving, and the final sentence of the poem, while ingenious, ends up sounding comparatively pat as a result.

I don't mean this as a dig at Hayes, whom I find to be as

reliably alert, imaginative, and entertaining a poet as just about anyone writing right now. Instead, it's a reminder for me of just how hard it is to stand amid so much motion, which seems better suited, I think, to a truly social occasion, one in which the play can continue as a shared and ongoing way of encountering each other—a collaboration—rather than a way to execute a series of movements that, in beginning, a poet promises to complete. Until those last four lines, the poem is alive—and Hayes, if elusive, is alive in that riffing, too. But there's no way to hand that off at the end, not, at least, without forgoing much of the freedom and delight that got it there. There's no satisfying way for the person who has been inclined to counter his each motion in order to move again to step forward and be recognizable as the person he has, until that final moment, been.

In this, contemporary poems that playfully court absurdity feel very different from much older poems that they otherwise have much in common with, those poems in which wit lodges itself not only in the movement of a recognizable mind but also in the expectations of a governing form. And so a poem like the first sonnet in Sidney's *Astrophil and Stella* ("Loving in truth and fain in verse my love to show"), which also arrives at its conclusion via a fast-moving slapstick—this one playing with outrageously mixed metaphors for trying to write—can also bring that movement to an abrupt halt at the end without undoing the terms by which it had moved:

> Thus great with child to speak and helpless in my throes,
> Biting my truant pen, beating myself for spite,
> "Fool," said my Muse to me, "look in thy heart, and write."

For a poem like "Woofer," there can be no such final twist into simplicity without the poet working against his implicit argument in favor of particularity and complexity (and in favor of pleasure, too). Which is not to say that Hayes should be writing in fixed forms. "Woofer" succeeds, as long as it succeeds, in different terms, the ability to come alive inside categorical identities that are insufficient to his delight, and to make their insufficiency into one of the sources of delight, even as he suggests that such terms are inevitable. It succeeds in animating a kind of complexity that would be out of place in "Loving in truth…" (which has its own complexity, and its own sources of delight) since the conventions Hayes wants to play with are meant to live (and critiqued in part for their inability to credibly live) more deeply in the life of a distinct individual and span more broadly into the particulars of the society as a whole. It intends, even in its absurdity, a kind of realism—a version of realism—that would have been inconceivable to Sidney. It intends something more flawed than mastery, no matter how masterful it may be.

Oh swirling petals, all living things are contingent,

Falling leaves, and transient, and they suffer.
But the Universal is the goal of jokes,
Especially certain ethnic jokes, which taper

Down through the swirling funnel of tongues and
        gestures
Toward their preposterous Ithaca.

The lines come fairly late in Robert Pinsky's beautiful, meandering elegy, "Impossible to Tell," a poem that tells multiple jokes but, like McDonough's, isn't primarily a humorous poem. Also like McDonough's, it isn't itself social but has much to say about the role of humor in our social lives. Like Hayes's, it's interested in the way that categorical identities both define and fail to describe our lives. (Also like Hayes's, it ends in a moment of resolution that doesn't, to my ear, sufficiently embody all the complexity that got it there.)

I'm not persuaded by Pinsky's claim that "the Universal is

the goal of jokes," not entirely. But I'm fascinated by its function in that sentence, how it becomes one part of the poem's veering through contingencies, with some of the same snap as the punch-line in a joke, and then becomes the set up for the next swerve (and how all of that swerving echoes Odysseus's own elaborate journeying as he longed, not without distraction, for his Ithacan home). And that overlap is, I think, a part of what Pinsky has in mind: the way joking, like storytelling, roots deep in human traditions, the way the forms persist, the way in our erasable particularity we long for something more lasting (though we want, at the same time, to preserve our particularity as well). Here's the joke Pinsky offers as evidence:

> In the Belgian Army, the feud
> Between the Flemings and Walloons grew vicious,
>
> So out of hand the army could barely function.
> Finally one commander assembled his men
> In one great room, to deal with things directly.
>
> They stood before him at attention. "All Flemings,"
> He ordered, "to the left wall." Half the men
> Clustered to the left. "Now all Walloons," he ordered,
>
> "Move to the right." An equal number crowded
> Against the right wall. Only one man remained
> At attention in the middle: "What are you, soldier?"
>
> Saluting, the man said, "Sir, I am a Belgian."
> "Why, that's astonishing, Corporal—what's your name?"
> Saluting again, "Rabinowitz," he answered:

Just before telling the joke, Pinsky writes, "I wish that I could tell it / To Elliot." It's a reminder that jokes belong to the living, a community Elliot Gilbert, whom the poem elegizes, has been taken from. It's a reminder of what the joke can't do, just as the punch-line itself undercuts the commander's optimism that a unified Belgian identity is possible—a hope shared only by the one man in the room least likely to be seen as Belgian by anyone else. If the poem reaches toward any universal, it's a universal knowledge of exclusion. The joke depends on an understanding of Jewishness as outsiderness, a reminder that the "universal" many jokes aspire to is as exclusive as the universals literary critics, professional and amateur alike, sometimes so confidently describe.

There *are* universals, of course—death, for instance, though we understand it in very different ways. And—although it's not *quite* universal—friendship, or at least the longing for it. Gilbert, the poem notes, "had in his memory so many jokes / They seemed to breed like microbes in a culture / Inside his brain." But the poem is, the epigraph notes, not only a memorial to Gilbert but also written to Robert Hass, about whom he notes, just before explaining how Gilbert died:

> In the first months when I had moved back East
> From California and had to leave a message
>
> On Bob's machine, I used to make a habit
> Of telling the tape a joke; and part-way through,
> I would pretend that I forgot the punchline,
>
> Or make believe that I was interrupted—
> As though he'd be so eager to hear the end
> He'd have to call me back. The joke was Elliot's,
>
> More often than not.

I said that "Impossible to Tell" isn't really social—by which I mean, it doesn't really act at any point like an interaction between two people. It is, instead, like most poems, openly putting on a show, creating an act that moves through time as a reliable medium but does not seem to be taking place in the time of its movement. It is, to put it another way, obviously artificial—and if all of our social life is at least a little artificial, it nonetheless depends for its depth on a sense of immediacy, of the form falling away in favor of awareness of the other person with whom we are engaged. And yet....

Pinsky's practice of telling jokes into Hass's answering machine and then stopping before he delivers the punchline is also a reminder that putting on a show for another is a kind of care, and has its own immediacy. The poem opens, just before it introduces Elliot:

> Slow dulcimer, gavotte and bow, in autumn,
> Bashō and his friends go out to view the moon;
> In summer, gasoline rainbow in the gutter,
>
> The secret courtesy that courses like ichor
> Through the old form of the rude, full-scale joke,
> Impossible to tell in writing. *"Bashō"*
>
> He named himself, "Banana Tree": banana
> After the plant some grateful students gave him,
> Maybe in appreciation of his guidance
>
> Threading a long night through the rules and channels
> Of their collaborative linking-poem
> Scored in their teacher's heart: live, rigid, fluid
>
> Like passages etched in a microscopic circuit.

The whole time I've been writing this essay, I've been thinking of my friend Sean. For almost 15 years, we mostly lived in the same place—first Southern California, then New York. Sean intimidated me when we first met. He seemed a little slick. His quick wit outran me. He seemed like a sophisticated adult when I still felt like an awkward child. I was uptight, anxious, stiff, judgmental. He was—I felt certain of it—the kind of person who would judge me for those things. That I was wrong about that last part is probably too obvious to dwell on. What's been on my mind here is how often, how hard, he made me laugh. And how awful his life was at the moment when I started feeling safe with him, and how important that sense of safety was in helping me learn to feel safe more often with others. And how, for a while, I valued the friendship less as that became more possible for me. Sean was—and is—an exceptional performer. It bothered me sometimes, at first: seeing how fast he read a room, each person an audience, and how quickly, how fully, how effectively, he bent himself toward what that person wanted from him, often before the person had even thought to want it. For a long time I missed the loneliness at the heart of it, of him. I missed, too, the courtliness of it, "The secret courtesy that courses like ichor," Pinsky writes.

For a few stanzas, "Impossible to Tell" delves into what seems like memoir, describing Pinsky's own beginnings as a performer:

> Imagine a court of one: the queen a young mother,
> Unhappy, alone all day with her firstborn child
> And her new baby in a squalid apartment
>
> Of too few rooms, a different race from her neighbors.
> She tells the child she's going to kill herself.
> She broods, she rages. Hoping to distract her,
>
> The child cuts capers, he sings, he does imitations
> Of different people in the building, he jokes,
> He feels if he keeps her alive until the father
>
> Gets home from work, they'll be okay till morning.
> It's laughter *versus* the bedroom and the pills.
> What is he in his efforts but a courtier?

Later in the poem, he admits, speaking of that child:

> Or maybe he became
> The author of these lines, a one-man *renga*
>
> The one for whom it seems to be impossible
> To tell a story straight.

It's hard to capture the feeling of that meandering in excerpts. The poem's movements are longer, the stories slower to return after they wander off stage. And of course all this ties in to the poem's title, which is also its refrain, and the implication that there is no sufficient way to remember Gilbert. But then again: "The movement // Of linking renga coursing from moment to moment / Is meaning, Bob says in his Haiku book." Maybe the actual goal of most jokes is movement, a circuit in which our essential medium, time, takes shape. Maybe the goal of most jokes is just pleasure—the pleasure of being in motion, a kind of athleticism, really, and the pleasure of giving someone else pleasure, too. Of moving someone, in a nearly literal sense of the term.

I think of how generous Sean was—and still is—in trying to heal himself through others. How little, besides our happiness, he asked of us in return. And I think of how unlikely it is, sometimes, the fluency that can take over a room, that all of our complexities can find a form in which we are all at once especially alive. The gift of that, even if it does not answer the appetites that make it possible. It's possible, I think, that part of the encounter with another in a poem, part of the person we find when we read, is simply that hunger to make something, and how that hunger must bend to reach us, to become something that can live in the circuits that can be inscribed on a page. So, too, with jokes, whose goal is also to usher us, however cloaked, however burdened, a little farther toward people we do and do not know.

"Signifying Nothing": On Confidence

It comes late in the play, the claim that language is too late: "There would have been a time for such a word." And with that, Macbeth launches into one of the most meaningful speeches about meaninglessness ever contrived.

The soliloquy betrays disdain for its own materials, a need to undo, through speech, all that might merit saying. Macbeth does his work of de-meaning in metaphors, those connective acts of borrowed meaning. And those metaphors all come from realms that insist on connections: chronology, illumination, theater, storytelling. Their artfulness argues against the very things they say.

Macbeth has his reasons. Most immediately, his wife has committed suicide, fleeing a mind stripped of every meaning save one: the guilt that she and her husband cannot wash away. Rather than erasing himself in turn, Macbeth attempts to erase the world.

Throughout the play, Macbeth aspires to silence, a silence that will be denied him: as soon as he finishes, a messenger arrives. But it's a silence in which he's had the last word. He has the confidence of the atheist who is angry with God. It is the confidence of the desperate, but it's confidence all the same.

⌇

Confident: *"with faith"* or *"with trust."* Though faith (or trust) in what, the word doesn't say.

Julia Kristeva begins *Black Sun*, her meditation on depression and art, "For those who are racked by melancholia, writing about it would have meaning only if writing sprang out of that very melancholia." The problem—her point—is that depression is incompatible with writing. More specifically, it's incompatible with words. She equates depression with what she terms *asymbolia*, a state of affairs that encompasses "unbelieving in language" and, more precisely, an impression of "the signifier's failure to insure a compensating way out of the states of withdrawal in which the subject takes refuge."

Macbeth doesn't suffer from this.

≋

With faith comes action—comes, at least, the possibility of action, a seamless sequencing of moments, each effect becoming a cause.

Hamlet, though, has a hard time with trust. In the play's first scene—one that's rife with rumor—Prince Hamlet's one true friend meets Hamlet's father (maybe), the murdered king (maybe, again).

If Hamlet's confidence in authority weren't sufficiently compromised by the death of his father and his mother's too-easy embrace of the new king in town, he also has to make sense of the instructions he gets from his maybe-father maybe-king, a man who, being dead, shouldn't be showing himself to Protestant England's untimely Danes. It's worth noting that this figure, according to Horatio, has usurped not only the night but the form—the power—of the once-living king, something Hamlet Jr. has notably failed to do, though no one (except Hamlet) ever dares mention it.

It's hard to say when *Hamlet* takes place. The mentions of Wittenberg suggest that we're in Shakespeare's present-day, Protestant country. But the story Shakespeare draws from is much older and belongs to that country's Catholic past. Scholars find evidence of both religions in the play, and no one ever actually says which faith they hold. It's tempting to say that the confusion is deliberate, another way Shakespeare involves his audience in the uncertain authority hovering over Hamlet throughout.

❧

Kristeva's explanation comforts me. There's relief in finding words that seem answerable to the silence into which I sometimes descend. It's even more of a relief because it is, itself, silent: static, private, manageable. Is it any wonder that poets often quote D.W. Winnicott? "It is a joy to be hidden but a disaster not to be found."

❧

Macbeth has his own unreliable messengers from the unlicensed beyond: the witches he imperfectly believes. Here, too, he batters at circumstance, murdering to bring about what they say would happen either way. Whether it actually would have, the play won't tell us. But Macbeth's attempt to act on his faithlessness turns out to be a very bad idea, in part because it demeans (and de-means) the approval that the prophecy might otherwise confer.

"To be thus is nothing," he laments, finding that the monarchy he has taken has left him human and exposed. "But to be safely thus." He doesn't finish the thought. Instead, he drifts toward awareness of his "fruitless crown," the feeling that he will now have to undo a prophecy (to Banquo: "Thou shalt get kings") entwined with the promise that he would ascend to the throne.

❧

Confiding is an act of trust—not only that someone will keep a secret but that she or he will understand your words, both what they mean and what they're for.

Hamlet ends the first of his many soliloquys by silencing himself as people approach: "But break," he instructs his heart, "for I must hold my tongue." Earlier in the same scene, he makes his first appearance on stage without a word. More than 60 lines pass before, finally addressed, he speaks (and even then his first line is an aside) and soon discovers that his one request (to leave) has been denied.

Hamlet is in large part a play about audiences and authority: who we listen to, who we talk to, what happens when we can't do either in a spirit of trust. So many of its metaphors have to do with eyes and ears—both the actual murder of King Hamlet and its later reenactment involve poison being poured into his ear. So much, including the ghost, must be seen to be believed. There are so many spies and messengers, almost all of them bad. And, of course, Hamlet stages a play just to watch the king watching it in order to confirm that the ghost has told him the truth. Once Hamlet knows—once Claudius knows he knows—Claudius has to send him away.

When Hamlet does start speaking, he engages in his own version of de-meaning. His is much more ripe than Macbeth's, full of puns and willful misreadings. It seems that Hamlet is attempting to inflate the already vacuous speech of the corrupt court with the reality of its corruption. It's at once amazing and unsatisfying. Hamlet seems to accept the adolescence that Claudius imposes by denying him the throne. He rejects Claudius' authority but doesn't claim his own, always keeping his meaning just beyond the possibility of rebuke.

There's no real audience for this resistance—except, possibly, the actual audience of the play. He's trying to keep his words from becoming actionable—to keep them just below the cusp of actual communication. If he does intend any action, it's through provocation. He partly wants, I suspect, to make Claudius expose himself as the usurper of King Hamlet's role. It's all resistance, only resistance—like Macbeth, Hamlet uses words to limit what can be said—but it may also be a way of keeping the *possibility* of speaking alive, at least to himself, at least in the hope that someone else will speak for him.

﹏

Writing in the *Los Angeles Review of Books*, the poet and scholar Lisa L. Moore looked back on the poetry of the American women's movement in the 1970s and 80s, noting "A new language, a shift in human consciousness: Lorde and Rich did not think these were tall orders, but merely what the women's movement expected of its poets, and what poets could deliver for the benefit of all." The article had much to say about how a meaningful political poetry might come about. Part of what it says, I think, is that the first step is imagining that it could. We speak, write, hear, and read in code while imagining otherwise. Art's power comes in part from what we assume art's for, as well as our ability to keep—both through the quality of the art and the vigor of its reception—that assumption aloft.

Consider, as another example, the Black Arts movement, which insisted that recognizably "black" language was artistically at least as viable as apparently "white" language. In his afterword to *The Collected Poems of Lucille Clifton*, Kevin Young writes, "Black Arts sought many things but above all a public poetry— one aware of its audience and even pitched at times toward a newfound audience that it was both meeting and making."

To put it a little differently: the poetry's political value grew out of its ability to create a community of black writers and readers who believed that such a community was valuable.

﹏

In *Macbeth* and in *Hamlet*, when we are asked to think about language and theater we're invited to be suspicious. Polonius is full of shit even when he's right; his rightness is a tool to manipulate his audience, rather than something to share. Lady Macbeth submits her husband to an ongoing master class in acting — one that is so bullying and effective that Macbeth eventually decides to instruct her in the same terms. Hamlet, conducting his own acting class, tells his actors to hold a "mirror up to nature," but he does so in the service of deceit. Indeed, he tells his mother, once they've achieved a measure of trust, that he is only "mad in craft." Both speech and acting exert control over others. It's a one-sided confidence. Lacking faith in others, these characters invest in their own ability to draw others away from the truth.

⌐

This is the part of depression that surprises me: that it insists on its own meaning. Depression carries with it a sense of wrongness. It's not a nothingness. True nothingness wouldn't be troubling. It wouldn't allow for anything separate from itself. But depression focuses the mind on an absence, a loss of meaning that carries with it the sense that meaning should exist.

When the web comic *Hyperbole and a Half* returned after almost a year and a half, its first new post, long and anxiously awaited by fans who'd watched the site go silent in the wake of a post titled "Adventures in Depression," was called "Depression Part Two."

There's a bit in there where the comic's author, Allie Brosh, writes about the challenge of dealing with the people who wanted to help her. "It would be like having a bunch of dead fish," she explains, "but no one around you will acknowledge that the fish are dead. Instead, they offer to help you look for the fish or try to help you figure out why they disappeared."

Those sentences are, I think, an image of the *asymbolia* Kristeva describes—a symbol, the dead fish, refused not only its meaning but its plain identity. They're also reminiscent of much in contemporary poetry. Which makes me wonder how much of our writing is an attempt to keep the possibility of communication alive, absent any correspondence between what people feel and what they imagine they can say.

If it were done when 'tis done, then 'twere well
It were done quickly. If th' assassination
Could trammel up the consequence and catch
With his surcease success, that but this blow
Might be the be-all and the end-all here,
But here, upon this bank and shoal of time,
We'd jump the life to come.

It's not that Macbeth doesn't want to kill the king. It's just that he doesn't want to be a person who has killed the king—the supposedly good king, the king who's a guest at his house. He wants to be the good king, and, unwilling to admit that such a thing is impossible, he goes on wanting it.

Macbeth wants to arrive at a place beyond harm. It's his fantasy of monarchy (an ironic one; he's already shown just how possible it is to harm a king). With each next risk of exposure, he imagines that one more murder will seal up the threat. He has murdered sleep and murdered communication; he murders the one man, Banquo, he had taken into his trust. In murdering the king, he devalues the very kingship he's willing to kill for, making it meaningless before he can make it his. He has even invited the audience gathered in the theater to wonder whether the words of the witches were true or simply another manipulation. As Banquo puts it, "to win us to our harm, / The instruments of darkness tell us truths."

Macbeth ends Act I by echoing the witches' confusion of fair and foul for the second time (the first allusion comes in his very first words of the play):

I am settled and bend up
Each corporal agent to this terrible feat.
Away, and mock the time with fairest show.
False face must hide what the false heart doth know.

Macbeth is schooling himself here with the same lesson in theatricality that Lady Macbeth will remind him of repeatedly throughout the course of the play. "Who dares receive it other," she has just asked, "As we shall make our griefs and clamor roar / Upon his death?" After Duncan's death, Malcolm and Donalbain realize, just as Hamlet does, that a roaring performance of grief is much more persuasive than grief's actual, untheatrical, juddering course through the tangle of a life.

❧

Doubt, we like to say, is essential to poetry. Having said it myself, I think I know what we mean: no bumper stickers, no greeting cards, no Thomas Kinkade paintings. No poems that run like an aqueduct rather than a river. No thinly superhuman elevations of the artist beyond the reaches of our mortal and muddled care. No art that arrives already foreclosed. No art whose designs on us override any possibility of our engagement.

But I doubt that I've ever loved a poem that lacked confidence. Take for example, Frank Bidart. Bidart is a poet of doubt whose writing assumes the importance of both poetry and doubt. Yet his almost-lifelong commitment to developing radical representations of the ways in which faith has failed him is only possible because he believes, and because he covninces me, that writing about it can be valuable.

❧

Two lines cut through a poem. One runs jaggedly across the page from the upper-left-hand corner to the lower-right— the poem's almost-inevitable chronology of one word after another. The other line runs in some more mysterious way between writer and reader, often passing through revisions, personas, printings, evaluations, publications, readings, distribution, and purchases along the way. The poem arrives at such a distance, even if that distance is only that of one person handing a poem to another, that it would be impossible to pull the line taut like a string between two cans.

But as we follow the poem from upper-left to lower-right, we are reimagining that other, longer, stranger line. Our movement through the poem represents the unlikely way in which words pass over the distance between two people, in spite of all that gets altered and lost in transit. It takes some energy, some confidence, to make that representation vital enough to merit our care. As a reader, I want the poet to do me the honor of assuming I'm out there. I want her to do me the honor of assuming I might care—as well as the honor of working hard to make sure that I do.

≫

My former professor, James McMichael, had a theory about puns. All jokes, he reasoned, require a victim. In the case of puns, that victim is the language itself—and the language, in this equation, exists by virtue of being heard. So the victim is the audience, and the only successful pun is the one that elicits a groan.

It worries me sometimes—not to the extent that it worries me, for instance, that bigotry persists and that it probably persists in me in ways I'm not aware of, but still, it worries me sometimes—that much of our writing about poetry insists on a need to disrupt language and the expectations woven into it. Such critical writing suggests disdain for an imagined audience at the same time that it courts a community of actual readers that's already in on the joke.

We want, we say, our poems to disrupt us, surprise us, *change* us, even. And some of the poetry that has come from those theories is extraordinary; some of it I learn from and love. But that rhetoric sometimes seems to dream of a poem that, in the name of doubt, moves beyond a confident reaching out toward an audience to an overconfident, condescending correction of one's audience through language that sounds one-sided and *over*confident, utopian—*dys*topian, almost.

⌐

It intrigues me that Shakespeare went to his audiences, the audiences that he depended on for his livelihood, audiences that even included the queen or king, with so much concern about the relationship between speakers and audiences, about authority in both senses of the word. He went to them with so many metaphors, presenting acting as deceit, theater as meaningless, ears as corruptible, language as manipulation, faces as falsehoods. Shakespeare even went so far as to present the very words (how often in *Macbeth* must a character insist that someone is worthy of the title or adjective he just used for that person?) as unreliable, in need of more and more words. It intrigues me that he did this in writing of extraordinary abundance: plays that are implausibly rich with action, ideas, characters, invention, allusion, and humor. These plays reach out to the very audiences they're warning about the relationship between anyone who speaks or acts and anyone who listens or sees. It intrigues me, too, that more than 400 years later, almost halfway through the standard life span of a language's continuity, the confidence of that reaching out continues to prove its own validity.[1]

⌐

---

1 And it makes me wonder, too, if his success in that regard benefits from, along with his genius, writing in a genre that made his audience so much more tangible, so much more visible, to him; and at a time when the relationship between poet and reader was so much more immediate, too, the poems still passing from hand to hand, in literal manuscripts; and, as well, from my arriving at his plays and his poems knowing, assuming, before I've cracked the spine, that this is important, this is great.

On a basic level, Hamlet does have what one might call faith. He's not an atheist. He takes for granted that, if he kills himself, he'll go to hell. He wishes that "the Everlasting had not fixed / His canon 'gainst self-slaughter," an assertion that gets him, for all that he expects it to work, about as close to prayer as anyone does in the play. But he later describes the world as "an unweeded garden," an image of neglect that diverges slightly, but tellingly, from Macbeth's much angrier suggestion of divine idiocy.

As in *Macbeth*, the king's killer tries to pray. And as in Macbeth, he fails. Hamlet, watching, believes that his uncle's prayer has power. He refrains from killing Claudius at that moment, because he assumes that Claudius *is* praying. He defers in the hope of later taking him "full of bread," just as his father was killed. But we get no indication that Hamlet, once he has finished with that first encounter with his father's ghost, considers prayer himself. The divine audience seems unavailable or inappropriate for his needs. Instead, he seeks his absent father, now a ghost.

He so wants to hear from his father that he is willing to follow his ghostly shade even if the apparition is, in fact, a demon leading him into hell. Meanwhile, among those he can summon, he finds no audience of real value. Hamlet speaks honestly (and, at first, clumsily, as if unused to it) only when alone or with people whose lack of royal standing makes them seem inconsequential to him. And for all that he mocks authority, Hamlet will not let his lessers forget that he is still a prince deserving of the respect ("my lord") that entails. There is an audience for Hamlet, but it's not the one he wants.

❧

I've been writing criticism for a while now, and I still struggle with the role. To say that a poem or book is "bad" is essentially to say it has no true value. And value, as far as I can tell, is really just the result of someone potentially valuing a thing. To say something is bad, I would have to first imagine all its possible uses, all of the different moments in all of the different lives and minds in which that book or poem might appear. It feels a little bit like proving a negative. I worry about the person I might be erasing with the judgment.

We do not know ourselves, not completely. We do not know each other. And yet we feel some need to move towards each other, if not through knowledge then through the hope of knowledge, the nervous hope of being known. We approach each other through kindness, literally — through recognizing the possibility of kinship, of being the same kind. We reach out indirectly, offering the hope of pleasure, meaning, offering gifts of our making, things we made for the pleasure of making and the hope of making something good. And, of course, we fail. As audiences, as authors, and as people, we fail.

In Stephen Booth's 1969 essay "On the Value of *Hamlet*," Booth calls *Hamlet* "the tragedy of an audience that can't make up its mind." I'm wondering if we can't go even further. Perhaps we can see the challenge of understanding Hamlet's inaction as an indication of Shakespeare's imaginative and inviting sympathy with an audience that must, when the play is over, live in a society of shifting and mutually exclusive authorities. Seen from this perspective, the play becomes his attempt to offer something of value to people trying to navigate a world in which authority has unsavory designs on its audience and many audiences seem unworthy of the trust that words require. I wonder if that isn't the real key to understanding Hamlet's famous delay, or, at least, understanding our fascination with it. It reflects both our fantasy of cutting through everything to the no-doubt flattering truth, and our reality of being clumsy, uncertain, and stuck.

That Shakespeare, living in the same situation, wrote *Hamlet*—a confident telling of a world where confidence has broken down—may not help much for those of us with no hope of ascending into the ranks of the world's great writers. But in as much as the desire to be loved or accepted or even heard will include a desire to do better, it seems like a useful model nonetheless. And to stand, to move, inside a world where not knowing who to trust, what to say, how to act, takes on such power, such abundance—that consoles me, too.

～

Admittedly, my response to Booth isn't very far from Booth; it's mostly just a shift of emphasis. Here's more from him:

> *Hamlet* refuses to cradle its audience's mind in a closed generic framework, or otherwise limit the ideological context of its actions. In *Hamlet* the mind is cradled in nothing more than the fabric of the play. The superior strength and value of that fabric is in the sense it gives that it is unlimited in its range, and that its audience is not only sufficient to comprehend but is in the act of achieving total comprehension of all the perceptions to which its mind can open. The source of the strength is in a rhetorical economy that allows the audience to perform both of the basic actions of the mind upon almost every conjunction of elements in the course of the play: it perceives strong likeness, and it perceives strong difference. Every intellectual conjunction is also a disjunction, and any two things that pull apart contain qualities that are simultaneously the means of uniting them.

～

As I try to wrap this up, my own confidence wanes again. Needing to justify all these words, I keep going back and worrying over earlier passages, adding new ones, trying to buttress the essay against judgment, trying to plug any possible leaks. After the pleasure of writing these thousands of words, I want to go silent. I want, very strongly, to hide. I want someone to come find this essay, this book, and approve—to offer proof of my validity—without my having to first stand behind it, without my having to hand it to someone and say I think this is worth your time. And then, in asking you for that, I realize I've made it harder for you to give it in any credible way. I realize I've made, as I often do in my social life, too much, and too little, of you. I've made "you" about me again.

I keep coming across research that suggests the value of our illusions. These studies make me nervous, in part because they often seem to have designs on us—looking for ways to get more production out of our pre-appraised time. But, of course, we almost always have designs of some sort on each other. To imagine otherwise is just to construct another illusion. And that's the other worry for me: how do we meet each other meaningfully in a world where we know that the truth won't always set us free?

More to the point, how do we speak, write, and respond to each other both in confidence and in the knowledge of our frailty? There is some knowledge that we must insist on—knowledge of harm, of bigotry, cruelty, torture, injustice, devastation, neglect. There are countless ways in which the circle of kindness remains too small, ways in which we exploit the frailty of others near and far. And yet the people I have met who manage to do the most about these very problems seem to me to be extremely optimistic—overly optimistic, I believe. So who am I, who does so much less, to insist on what I see as the truth?

I do believe that kindness begets kindness. I also believe

in the value of seeing and creating complexity, in the kind of conversation that requires distinction to connect, though maybe this is just another of my own cherished illusions. I imagine that both values can be held simultaneously—and, yes, confidently. This occurs not through any stable set of aesthetic values but through an ongoing recognition of our shifting identities and ongoing vulnerability, our hope for improvement and our continuing, shared, reality of failure. And I believe—I have faith—that continuing to engage in that process honestly and caringly (and, of course—*of course*—with room for disagreement) creates the potential for richer, more inclusive communication.

Just as religious faith requires sacrifice and encompasses doubt, the confiding of any literary endeavor requires us to attempt, in uncertain terms, the difficult rhyming of unlikeness through the vulnerability that life (*meaningful* life, *honest* life) requires of us. It forces us to say to a stranger who is not present, *Here. This is for you. I've done the best that I can.* And to say it with the confidence required to make it true.

Epilogue

Talk of timeless poetry makes me anxious. There's a loneliness floating loose inside the phrase as I hear it, the poems
having gradually let go their particulars as they drift out of
our orbit, gone silent somewhere far out in deep space. It's
just a figure of speech, of course. No one expects poems to
outlive humanity, as far as I can tell, although it's possible—if
not at all comforting—that one day our robot overlords or
cyborg analogues will stand on some other planet orbiting
some other sun at some different rate and listen to Beowulf
with awe and delight.

Hanging out with my friend Matthew, for whom the idea
of timelessness is a consolation, I try for a different figure.
Timelessness, I say, doesn't really speak to difference (though
he disagrees; this, for him, is exactly what it does). What if we
talk (I'm not listening very closely now; he'll have to remind
me of his objections later on) about a poem's ability to work
as a metaphor—as something whose similarity is made meaningful by difference, whose difference is made meaningful
by similarity? Though Matthew's still skeptical (among other
things, he's pretty sure I should be using the term "analogy")
the idea appeals to me. It feels more flexible, less grand, more
like one potential virtue among many, less binary. (And less
like a handle we can use to grasp a future about which we
know nothing and beat each other over the head.)

And so maybe we can talk about a poem's reach—its
potential as a metaphor, wherein one life, real or imagined,
can achieve greater significance, in one regard, by its ability
to connect to a reader across greater measures of difference,
including that of time (though maybe not privileging time
over other distances). If the cyborgs do read Beowulf, part
of their pleasure, part of its power for them, will surely be
rooted in the time the poems will have passed through on
their way to them, the mortality those poems will have carried

over centuries and millennia, past thousands of suns. Their awe and delight will likely include awareness of just how many things time has changed since someone, at one specific time, wrote down these words that still speak, literally and figuratively (though differently, too), to them.

Matthew had been making a different point before I got us into this—that there's something of importance still lingering inside that terrible word, "relatable." I think he's right, though it makes both of us a little uneasy. We've both taught high school—and we're both humans, which means we can be arrogant, and we're both straight, white, cis males who grew up in economic comfort, which means the world is often happy to help our arrogance along. "Relatable" generally works as a way of pressing down on the edge of the universe closest to you, insisting that all things roll in your direction and dismissing anything that doesn't as warped or broken or weird or hard or too concerned with "identity." But he's right, I think: poems are meant to be encounters. They are, to state the obvious, things that people write for other people to read. They are a kind of relationship.

That's part of what first made poetry matter for me. At a time in my life when I was especially lonely, I found company in poems. They were a place to meet people in terms that yielded significance. And they still matter for me (and, I think, for many others, too) in a way that depends on the awareness that they were written by other human beings in the hope that other people would meet them there.

I am no more comfortable saying that all people should value poems in these terms than I am in saying that all people should live, dress, think or act like I do. I'm not even comfortable with the idea that more people should care about poetry. William Carlos Williams' lines, from "Asphodel, That Greeny Flower," make a popular case for poems:

It is difficult
to get the news from poems
yet men die miserably every day
for lack
of what is found there.

The common and, I suspect, correct interpretation of those lines is that "what is found there" is found only there—that Williams finds (and we should find) some cure for miserable death in poems that is only available there. I don't buy that, and not so much because miserable deaths can just as easily visit those who have spent a lifetime reading poems as those who haven't. (Williams, a doctor, surely knew as much; I'm fine with taking that as another figure of speech.) I just don't think poetry works for everyone; I don't think it's meaningful, or valuable, or beautiful, for everyone. And I don't think *poetry* is the point. People are. And sometimes, for some of us, a poem gives something. Sometimes, a person, in making a poem, gives something to another person. One life, through this incredibly complex circuit, whose complexity is one of the things it gives, becomes relatable to another, as mine does with my wife, or my parents, or my brother, or a friend. A relationship lights up the language between them. Someone is made less lonely, more alert, given pleasure, given sorrow and the means to carry it, made more, however momentarily, alive. Yes. Yes.

Publication Notes:

"Praise the Mutilated World": On Joy was originally published
by *LitHub*.

"Who Know in Singing Not to Sing": On Decorum was originally
published by *Kenyon Review*.

"Impersonations of Ordinary": On Humility was originally published
by *The American Poetry Review*.

"All We Can Say": On Politics was originally published
by *Kenyon Review Online*.

"Signifying Nothing": On Confidence was originally published
by *The Los Angeles Review of Books*.

Acknowledgments

My debts run too wide and deep to account for all of them here, but a few public thanks nonetheless:

To Dan Kois, who decided I should be a critic, then taught me the art and gave me an audience.

To Sumita Chakraborty and Matthew Buckley-Smith, whose careful reading of this book improved it considerably—and taught me to think and write more carefully.

To Gabrielle Calvocoressi, for support and encouragement that helped me to carry on when I was ready to give up, and for her example, and for inspiring the chapter on joy.

And to Kaveh Akbar and francine j. harris, who, along with Gaby, created a small, extraordinary, brief community (and a podcast) that was a second home for me, and with whom I developed the ideas and questions that turned into the chapter on politics.

To Belle Boggs, for encouraging me to write the chapter on confidence, and for helping me to become more confident in what I wrote.

To David Baker, for his extraordinary guidance and support.

To Alan Shapiro, for his extraordinary guidance and support, and for teaching me how to think seriously about poems almost a quarter-century ago.

To Michael Taeckens, for his support of this book.

To Kimberly Verhines, Sarah Johnson, and everyone at Stephen F Austin State University Press.

To Richard Allen, Ryan Wilson, Robert von Hallberg, Penelope Pelizzon, and Darcie Dennigan for opportunities and ideas along the way.

To Jeff, Mary, and Ed Farmer, for a lifetime of love and acceptance.

And to Caroline Luther, for all my days. For you.

About the Author

Photo Credit: Caroline Luther

Jonathan Farmer is the editor-in-chief and poetry editor of *At Length*, and he has frequently written about poetry for Slate.com, *The Kenyon Review*, and *Los Angeles Review of Books*. He teaches middle and high school English, and he lives in Durham, NC.

CPSIA information can be obtained
at www.ICGtesting.com
Printed in the USA
FFHW021345230419
51953597-57358FF